My humble *praNAms* and congratulations for a fantastic work done. It is going to be useful as long as humans live on this earth.
Professor V. Krishnamurthy, well-known Advaita scholar

It is a pleasure to acknowledge Dennisji's 'labor of love' and his trusting me with the task of making a few helpful hints along the way. As the Gita assures us, no good deed ever goes to waste, and even if human beings ignore this work, Dennisji will be blessed for it.
Sunder Hattangadi, moderator for Advaitin Elist, Sanskrit scholar

What a great work!
Alan Jacobs, president, Ramana Maharshi Foundation UK, and well-known author

This lovely book provides two levels of Sanskrit instruction. It is a wonderful guide to all those individuals that would like to know the basic Sanskrit religious vocabulary and how to read, write, and pronounce Sanskrit terms. The book introduces the transliterated Sanskrit alphabet and secondly, it teaches the Devanagari script/alphabet. The second level also teaches the main rules for combining Sanskrit letters and words – which is often a headache for the beginner. Many examples are provided from the Hindu scriptures to illustrate these two levels of teaching. As well, there is a comprehensive glossary of the most commonly encountered spiritual terms. This useful book will appeal to all serious spiritual seekers interested in the Hindu scriptures and Sanskrit terminology. Its aim is to teach the reader so as to be able to look up Sanskrit words in a dictionary and to write and pronounce them correctly. I am sure that all 'beginners' or even more advanced seekers of Hindu wisdom will find this a wonderful guide.

John Grimes, author of *A Concise Dictionary of Indian Philosophy*

Sanskrit
for
Seekers

Sanskrit
for
Seekers

Dennis Waite

MANTRA
BOOKS

Winchester, UK
Washington, USA

First published by Mantra Books, 2014
Mantra Books is an imprint of John Hunt Publishing Ltd., Laurel House, Station Approach,
Alresford, Hants, SO24 9JH, UK
office1@jhpbooks.net
www.johnhuntpublishing.com
www.mantra-books.net

For distributor details and how to order please visit the 'Ordering' section on our website.

Text copyright: Dennis Waite 2013

ISBN: 978 1 78279 227 7

A CIP catalogue record for this book is available from the British Library.

Design: Stuart Davies

Printed and bound by CPI Group (UK) Ltd, Croydon, CR0 4YY

We operate a distinctive and ethical publishing philosophy in all
areas of our business, from our global network of authors to
production and worldwide distribution.

CONTENTS

Acknowledgments

I would like to dedicate this book to the memory of Peter Bonnici, a dear friend who died on 22nd June 2013. Peter carried out a thorough review of the first edition of this text and made many corrections and suggestions. These changes have improved the book very significantly.

Introduction

So, why would you want to learn Sanskrit? Unless you are one of those fortunate few who have a genetic disposition for language learning or unless you are unfortunate enough to have a masochistic streak, why on earth would you want to tackle such an apparently formidable language? It shares with Latin the characteristic of having to change the ending of words depending upon the role of a noun or upon who is the subject of a verb and its tense. In fact, it is even worse than Latin. In Latin there is only singular and plural number, whereas Sanskrit has singular, two, and more than two!

It really must be almost impossible to learn this language unless you begin at school. I only wish that I had had the opportunity and studied it instead of Latin! Unfortunately, I didn't and it's certainly too late to start now; I often have difficulty remembering what I read yesterday!

Before continuing, I may as well confirm the implied and appalling admission above: I know very little Sanskrit! I cannot construct sentences or even decline nouns or conjugate verbs. I can just about read the script. I can sometimes split words into their parts or put them together – but would almost always have to refer to other sources for assistance in this. I could write the script, very clumsily, if I had to, providing I could refer to a list of the characters or to this book. But, let's face it, why would I want to? You need not just any italic pen, but one with a sloping nib, for goodness' sake! With free software on the Internet to convert transliterated Roman characters into the Sanskrit script, there is not really any need. What then, you may justifiably ask, gives me the credentials (or temerity) to write a book about Sanskrit? Well, I hope that by the time you finish reading this short introduction, you will know and accept the answer. Basically, I was – and to a degree still am – in the same position that you are.

Sanskrit is a very beautiful language. You only need to look at the flowing, cursive, perfectly proportioned script to see this, even if you cannot yet even determine where one word ends and another begins. And, when you learn about some of its other peculiarities, you will appreciate this even more. For example, once you learn how to pronounce a particular letter, you will know how to pronounce it in every word you will ever encounter. There are not many languages which could make that claim!

Perhaps the most amazing aspect is the almost mathematical precision with which letters and syllables combine. One name that you will find invariably associated with the language is Panini – he constructed a complex set of rules, which may be memorized through short 'sutras'. These enable one to work out how to assemble words and syllables into sentences. So impressive and logical is this set of rules that NASA have apparently proposed it as the basis for a new computer language (see http://post.jagran.com/NASA-to-use-Sanskrit-as-computer-language-1332758613).

But none of this addresses the original question. What prompted you to pick up this book (and me to write it)? If it really is the case that you want actually to *learn* the language, then please put this book back on the shelf. There is an excellent two-volume work for learning the language written by Thomas Egenes (Ref. 6). What is more, Part 1 is available for free at http://www.scribd.com/doc/32874508/Introduction-to-Sanskrit-by-Thomas-Egenes so that you can try it out before committing.)

I suggest (hope) that your interest in this book comes from the fact that your actual interest is in Hindu scriptures such as the Upanishads and the Bhagavad Gita and maybe even the works of Shankara and other writers on non-duality. The fact is that, up until a few hundred years ago, all books and academic texts in India were written in Sanskrit. In this respect, it is similar to Latin in the West, except that Sanskrit is much more tenacious.

Whereas Latin really could be said to be dead now, Sanskrit is still very much alive in the field of spiritual study. Although it is not really spoken any longer (apart from the odd commune-style efforts), it is still written. Even today, books are being published which are entirely in Sanskrit!

The point is that traditional teaching (certainly in the philosophy of Advaita, which is my own specialization) always refers back to the original scriptural texts for its authority. This is because those scriptures are the actual source of knowledge for key truths regarding the nature of reality and of ourselves. This knowledge is simply not accessible by any other means. We cannot *see* God or infer that the visible universe is not in itself real but depends upon something more fundamental. These things have to be told to us, by someone in whom we can trust, until such time as we can realize those truths for ourselves.

Scriptures have an inherent problem – their brevity. For several thousand years, some of the oldest texts – the Upanishads and the Vedas of which they form a part – were passed on orally; there were no written versions. Accordingly, they had to be relatively short and memorable. They were chanted aloud repeatedly to ensure that they were passed down the generations without distortion or loss. Even today, traditional teachers and their disciples chant the mantras before the guru translates and explains their meaning.

Accordingly, some interpretation is almost invariably required by the seeker before he or she can grasp what is being said. And, as you may know, there are not merely different emphases in meaning by different teachers but totally different schools of philosophy claiming to be supported by the same scriptural texts. It follows that one is certain to encounter different translations of the same text. An obvious example is that the Bhagavad Gita is regarded as the 'bible' of the Hare Krishna movement, which is essentially dualistic (dvaita). Yet this same text has an authoritative commentary by Shankara and is revered by Advaitins.

Ideally, of course, one would only study Advaita, or any other philosophy/teaching methodology, under the guidance of a competent teacher who fully understands the scriptures and how to 'unfold' them (and is also fluent in Sanskrit!). Practically speaking, however, few seekers in the West have access to a qualified teacher and so are obliged to read such material themselves. Without any knowledge at all of Sanskrit, one simply has to hope that one has selected an 'appropriate' translation, and will not be misled by the choice of words. Unfortunately, this can be dangerous!

It would be possible, and maybe both interesting and instructive, to take a single verse from an Upanishad and examine the translations given by a selection of different authors. But it would also take quite a lot of space (and time and effort) to do this in detail. Suffice to say that, for example, the commentaries of a teacher from the lineage of Swami Chinmayananda will almost certainly differ in some key areas from those written by a teacher in the Ramakrishna/Vivekananda lineage. This is because the latter has incorporated elements from outside of Shankara's Advaita school. For example, they will maintain that profound meditation (*samAdhi*) can lead to enlightenment, whereas Shankara would insist that meditation is an action, which is not opposed to ignorance, and that only Self-knowledge can bring enlightenment.

Consequently, if one is reading a particular translation and commentary, and one encounters a statement which seems not to be in accord with one's prior understanding, it often becomes necessary to check the meaning of key words and see if the particular translation given has been biased. In order to be able to do this, a certain minimum level of understanding is needed.

This book provides that 'minimum level' (and no more!). You will not be able to read, write or understand Sanskrit *sentences* after reading this book. But you will, with a little effort, be able to read and understand Sanskrit *words*. And that, hopefully, will allow you to read commentaries on scriptures and look up the meaning of words with which you are unfamiliar. With this ability, you will hopefully move forward more quickly on your chosen spiritual path.

And even if you only read the postings of discussion groups on the Internet, or articles or blogs at my own website for example, you will find that some writers invariably take it for granted that you will be familiar with certain Sanskrit terms and they will use them gratuitously without providing any translation. If you have the patience and really want to follow such writing, you will have to look up the words that you don't know. Mostly, the Sanskrit in such cases will be transliterated so you just have to be familiar with ITRANS or the use of diacritical marks on letters (all explained within). But sometimes, a writer will expect you to know the Devanagari script itself and not even bother to provide transliteration, let alone translation. Probably you will give up at that point and simply feel sorry for (or irritated by) the author's superior attitude but, if you really want to proceed, this book should provide the help you need to persevere.

As an example, what would you make of the following two words if you encountered them?

मोक्ष
निर्वाण

Presumably not a lot. Yet, if you are a 'spiritual seeker', such words will be central to your life – the very goal of your existence. In addition, most of the original source material about them will have been written in Sanskrit. The first of these words usually appears as 'moksha' in English books on the subject. It literally means 'release from worldly existence', liberation from the ignorance that binds us to the illusions of our lives. In the context of Advaita, a better translation is simply 'freedom from Self-ignorance' or even 'gaining of Self-knowledge'. But how do you pronounce it? Probably, as I once did, you will say 'mocksha', with the 'o' sounding as in the word 'clock'. In fact, one should sound it like the 'oa' in 'cloak'. The second word is the goal of Buddhists, usually written 'nirvana'. It means 'absolute extinction of individual existence or of all desires and passions'. Probably your pronunciation of this is not too bad – you may have come across the 1970s pop group of this name. The accent is on the second syllable, which is a long 'a', as in 'bar', while the final 'a' is short as in 'cat'. If you are British as opposed to American, however, the 'v' may well be pronounced as 'w'.

Ideally, you would like to know all of these things but without actually having to learn the language. Up to a point, this is possible and it is the purpose of this book to provide the necessary background. This claim is possible because these were precisely the requirements that I had and which I have achieved to my own satisfaction.

This book effectively provides for three levels of attainment. First, it will teach you the two most commonly used 'transliterated' forms of the language. This word refers to an 'Anglicized', or more correctly 'Romanized', form of Sanskrit i.e. one that uses the alphabet with which we are already familiar. True Sanskrit is written in a script that bears no resemblance to English, has quite different letters, and requires rather more effort to learn. One of these transliterated forms – usually just called 'Roman' – is used in many books that utilize Sanskrit terms. This form has dashes and dots over or under letters to indicate how to pronounce them. They actually *are* different letters in the Sanskrit! As these are not available to the average typist, the second transliterated form, most frequently used on the Internet, is called ITRANS. (Unfortunately, quite a few books do not use any formal transliteration at all. These, instead, make crude attempts to reproduce Sanskrit words phonetically and often do not even bother to do this.)

With the knowledge of these two, it will be possible to look up words in any dictionary that does not use the actual Sanskrit script. The glossary of this book aims to provide explanations for many of the terms that you are likely to encounter in Western books on Eastern philosophy. You will also be able to use (or download) dictionary facilities on the Internet to look up words that are not provided here, and an explanation will be given as to how to go about this.

For those whose ambitions are a little higher, whose need is to be able to use a full Sanskrit–English dictionary to look up words, it is necessary to learn the Sanskrit alphabet, together with the original script that is used to reproduce it, and some basic rules for combining letters. This is the second level of attainment that will be addressed. While the first level may be achieved very easily, this higher level requires rather more effort. Suggestions are made as to how to achieve this, and pointers are given to free resources on the Internet that will prove helpful.

If the word that you wish to look up is actually in the dictionary, these first two steps will be adequate. Unfortunately, there are two main reasons why the word that you want to look up will not be in the dictionary:

1) The word in the text will have the ending appropriate to its part of speech or tense, whereas the dictionary only lists the forms before they have been declined or conjugated. (Unfortunately the scope of this book does not include the topics of declension or conjugation.)

2) Words in Sanskrit combine with adjacent words in many situations and the letters at the join frequently change. The consequence of this is that the separate words that make up a 'word' found in a book may not be immediately recognizable. In order to be able to separate out the book word into its constituent parts, a third level of

attainment is required – to learn the rules for joining. The last part of this book will introduce you to some of the main rules of so-called 'sandhi'.

The principal problem of course is the alien nature of the script. In order to be able actually to learn the alphabet in its original form, it is necessary to learn to recognize the form of each letter. Ideally, you would practice writing these yourself in order to help commit the letters to memory. None of this is intrinsically difficult but it does all take time.

In order to achieve the 'level 1' ability to pronounce and look up Romanized words in a glossary, you can expect to have to spend just a few hours reading the relevant parts of this book a couple of times. In order to be able to achieve 'level 2' ability, reading the actual script and looking up words in a Sanskrit–English dictionary, you must expect to spend several hours per week for a few months, with serious practice most days. You need not see this as a chore, however. This book aims to introduce the letters very gradually and present words for practice at the earliest opportunity. If you choose to use writing as an aid to learning, the script has great beauty and giving one's full attention in calligraphy is itself a useful practice for stilling the mind. If you wish to go further and learn all of the rules for joining words, this will require serious study, together with the assistance of someone who can provide the solution after you have given up! This book will only provide you with a good idea of what is involved – far more interesting and rewarding than crosswords or solving cryptograms!

Any genuine spiritual aspirant will want to make this effort. Your reward will be to be able to verify for yourself the correct pronunciation and meanings of words. You will no longer be at the mercy of the authors, translators or editors of the books you read. You will no longer be worried that you have misunderstood the meaning of a term used in an Internet email discussion group or heard from a teacher. You will be able to check the original source material for yourself and look up the meanings of key words.

This book will not address anything beyond these simple aims. It will not tell you how to decline nouns or conjugate verbs. These terms are not even defined, in case you do not know what they mean! You will not discover how to construct sentences or all of the rules for combining words. In other words, this book will not teach you the language in even its most basic form. Suggestions will be given, however, to those daring few whose ambitions do stretch that far.

General Introduction to the Language

True Sanskrit uses an alphabet quite unlike ours. For a start, it contains nearly twice as many letters overall, with more than three times the number of vowels. These letters can look quite different depending upon where they appear in a word and which other letters are adjacent. The language is written in a script called 'Devanagari' (meaning 'city of the gods').

It is an extremely interesting language and amazingly logical. There are many rules but, once you have learned them, there are none of the tiresome exceptions found in most languages. In addition, once you have learned how to pronounce a letter, it is *always* pronounced in that way.

It is interesting to note in passing that there is a close parallel between the structure of the language and the Sankhya-related myth of the creation. Indeed, some schools of thought, notably in the north of India and Kashmir, believe that the universe was 'spoken' into existence. Though this 'primordial' language is beyond ordinary sound, Sanskrit is its earthly manifestation, as it were, and embodies many of the 'universal principles'. The language itself is believed to embody the truth of the unity of the Self.

The entire language evolves from a fundamental sound. The laws governing the way that words are constructed, and the grammar used to join them, are strict. It is amazing that the language, though the most ancient known and no longer in general usage, remains true to its original form. Someone learning it now would be able to communicate perfectly well with someone who spoke the language thousands of years ago.

Level 1 The Transliterated Alphabet

Before introducing the Devanagari script, we will learn the basic alphabet in its transliterated form. All of the words in the 'Dictionary of Common Sanskrit Spiritual Words' (provided towards the end of this book) are given in this form and ordered as if the letters were English so that there is not actually any need for you to learn the real Sanskrit characters or alphabet order if you do not wish to. Rather than presenting this section twice – once for each of the transliterated forms – I will give both forms now for each letter, as it is introduced. These are, in any case, often the same. Note, however, that I will generally only show the ITRANS form when giving examples of Sanskrit words.

As was noted in the Introduction, the Romanized form is still used in most written material. This includes serious books and documents on the Internet held in, for example, postscript or Adobe® 'PDF' format. The reason that ITRANS was developed is that the Romanized form uses various 'diacritical' marks that are not easily available to someone typing on an ordinary computer keyboard. He or she must make use of the ordinary fonts provided with word processors, for storing and communicating the resultant data on or via computers. 'Diacritical' marks are modifications to basic letter forms. An example outside of Sanskrit would be the accents used in French – acute, grave, circumflex, and cedilla – é, è, ê, and ç. In the Romanized transliteration of Sanskrit, there are a number of special marks, such as lines (called macrons) over vowels, for example – ā. In order to be able to type and send this character easily, ITRANS writes it as 'aa' or 'A' but I will use 'A' throughout as this has now become the favored option of Internet users. The ITRANS scheme uses only the usual letters of our alphabet, together with the occasional special character such as the tilde ~. The special characters of ITRANS always appear as separate characters, however, and not over or under other letters as they do in Romanized transliteration.

In the last few years, it has become easier to reproduce the Roman forms via computers. For example, the Wordpress system, commonly used for hosting blogs on the Internet, has free plug-ins such as IndicIME (http://www.vishalon.net/IndicResources /IndicIME.aspx) to make entering languages with diacritical marks easy. Also the changeover to Unicode character encoding systems on websites has vastly expanded the number of different letter forms possible. This has meant that Romanized transliteration is found increasingly frequently in articles and web pages online. Nevertheless, because ITRANS has been used for so long now in emails and discussion groups, and because it is so easy to use, it is likely to remain popular for a long time yet.

It must also be noted that the pronunciation I will be describing is principally that recommended by the School of Economic Science, which represents the largest body of Sanskrit students in the UK. The development of their system is very clear and logical and therefore easy to learn and understand. Although all traditions generally agree in most respects, there are key differences regarding some elements. Since the vast majority of any communication you are likely to have will be written rather than verbal, this should present no problem, however. The main difference that would be noticed by anyone learning the language in the USA is that the 'v's are pronounced as 'v' there, whereas the logically correct pronunciation is 'w'. This will be explained in due course!

A. The Five Basic Vowels

1. a, a

The first letter of the alphabet forms the fundamental sound from which all others are derived simply by moving the tongue and lips. You make it by opening the mouth wide and letting the vocal cords operate. The sound which emerges sounds like a cross between the short 'a' in 'cat' and 'u' in 'but'. It is written as '*a*' in both of the transliterated forms but the correct letter in the Devanagari script is:

अ

(I will not show the Devanagari for any of the other letters, until the second part of the book.) In this first section, on the transliterated alphabet, I will show each letter as it is introduced in first the ITRANS form and then the Romanized form. Thus, the first letter is:

a, a

i.e. there is no difference for this letter. The fonts used in this book are: normal 11 point Times New Roman font for the basic text; 11 point Arial Unicode MS for the ITRANS and Romanized transliteration. The fonts used for the Devanagari script are 18 point Sanskrit 98 and 18 point ancientsanskrit99 for some special characters. Note that any special fonts used in the manuscript for this book, including the Devanagari script, may be downloaded free of charge from the Internet. Information about this will be provided later.

This, then (a, a), is the first letter of the alphabet and the first vowel or, to use its correct term, *svara*, meaning 'sound'. Its literal meaning is 'self-shining', to indicate that these are the only letters with sound. The consonants have no sound of their own and need to be combined with vowels to be 'manifest'. Unless we attach a vowel, the consonant is only throat and tongue position combined with an inner effort – there is no actual sound. By convention, *a* is always pronounced after each consonant (when we are speaking it as a letter) so as to enable the consonant sound to be manifest.

When we speak an English consonant, we also have to introduce a vowel before or after it in order to make a sound. For example, when we speak the letter 'm' we effectively say 'em'. It is never possible to speak a consonant without doing this, however slightly. When we speak the letter 'b', the expressed vowel comes after the word and we say 'be'; with 'k', we say 'kay', and so on. (Note that Sanskrit consonants are not invariably sounded with *a* when they occur in a word. Obviously they can be followed by other vowels! Also, a consonant at the end of a word or at the beginning of a conjunct consonant will not be sounded with *a*. These will be explained later.)

A word such as *aham*, meaning 'I', is an example of the use of *a*. (I will give a simple or useful example with each letter to help put it into context and aid memory.)

2. i, i

If the back of the tongue is now raised slightly towards the back of the roof of the mouth, keeping the front of the tongue down against the back of the lower teeth, and the same short movement of the vocal cords is made, a slightly different sound emerges. This sounds a bit like the short 'i' in 'bit'. It is written:

i, i

The word *iti*, meaning 'thus', is an example. It is frequently used in the scriptures to add stress to what has just been said.

3. R^i or RRi, ṛ

The next two vowels may seem strange but follow the logic of the development. The underlying sound for both of these is the '*i*' sound just covered but the tongue is first moved further forward in the mouth. If you raise the tip of the tongue until it is almost touching the roof of the mouth and then make the 'i' sound as before, the next vowel sound emerges. Modern students often actually flick the tongue downwards as the sound is made so that the result sounds something like 'ri' in the word 'rip'. Strictly speaking, the rolling 'r' beginning is not clearly enunciated because the tongue never actually touches the roof of the mouth. However, this articulation is not correct. The way in which it is written in the two forms of transliteration now differs clearly. In ITRANS, the special character '^' (caret) was used in the early versions, but is one which is nevertheless easily produced from the normal typewriter keyboard. In Romanized form, a dot is used beneath the letter:

ṛ

In the latest version of ITRANS, an alternative form is available that does not use any special character, namely:

RRi [Note that the free software utilities mentioned later, for generating Devanagari script, recognize both forms but RRi is the preferred form in the digital dictionary referred to later, so I will use this form preferentially.]

One of the oldest, if not the oldest, of the Upanishads is the Brihadaranyaka. This is a typical Anglicized spelling, which is in fact quite inaccurate. I will not jump ahead by giving you the full, correct spelling (look in the Glossary if you must!) but the first vowel in the word is this one so that the beginning is *bRRihad-.* Incidentally, it is convenient to tell you at this point that there is no distinction between capitals and lower case in Sanskrit – there is just the one case. In the Roman alphabet, having learned 26 lower-case letter forms, you then have to learn another 26 for the same letters in upper case. There is none of this in Sanskrit, which makes up to some extent for the fact that there are nearly as many *different* letters altogether and these often change their form in different situations!

4. L^i or LLi, ḷ (Note that the Roman form here is a lower-case letter 'el' with a dot under, not a capital I, nor a number 1, nor an exclamation mark !)

For the next of the principal vowels, this procedure is repeated but now the tip of the tongue moves further forward still, to just behind the front teeth, before the 'i' is sounded. Again, modern speakers often flick the tongue up towards the roof and down so that the sound that actually comes out is 'lri'. Again, this is not strictly correct but it hardly matters since there are very few words in the language that use this letter! The ITRANS form again may use the '^' symbol and the Romanized form the dot below the letter: LLi, ḷ

As before, the more recent releases of ITRANS allow the form '*LLi*' to be used and this is the form that will be used here, subsequently. The word *LLi* means 'mountain'.

5. u, u

Continuing the development, the emphasis finally shifts to the lips (labial position), having begun in the throat (guttural position), moved to the back of the mouth (palatal), then to the roof of the mouth (cerebral) and then to the teeth (dental). If a circle is formed of the lips but without any tension and the basic sound is made, a short 'oo' sound comes out as in 'soot' or 'put'.

This is the last of the simple vowels and is written the same in both transliterated forms:

u, u

This is, of course, the vowel that begins the word 'Upanishad' but this word is an Anglicized version since, as you will discover, the 'sh' part is actually a single letter in Sanskrit. Also remember, there should not actually be a capital letter. You should not worry too much about this latter aspect though. It is normal to use a capital where one would be used in English. This is especially the case (no pun intended) where a proper name is involved. It would be most unusual to come across the name Arjuna or, even more so, the name of a god, given in transliterated form without a capitalized first letter. If you are using Devanagari script, of course, the need to be aware of this etiquette disappears.

B. The Five Main Groups of Consonants

Before continuing to describe the other vowels, I will now switch to tell you about some of the consonants. The five vowels just described with their characteristic mouth positions effectively head up the five main groups of five consonants in each group. Consonants all effectively still sound the basic 'a' but 'stop' it from coming out in that simple way by varying the position of the tongue and lips in the way dictated by the vowel at the head of the group. The Sanskrit term for consonants is *vya~njana*, meaning a 'decoration' (of the basic vowel sound) but you will have to wait until later to find out how to pronounce this word.

I will attempt to describe how to sound the letters in each of these groups by appropriate positioning of the tongue and lips and use of the throat. However, a reviewer of this book pointed out a much simpler and more general 'rule' to bear in mind. That is to consider the mouth positioning required in order to pronounce English words beginning with the corresponding semi-vowel. (These will be described later.)

Thus, one can pronounce the guttural letters by having the tongue in the position required for pronouncing the 'h' of 'happy'. When the tongue is in the position needed for pronouncing the 'y' of 'yellow', it is also in the position for pronouncing the palatals. The tongue positioned to say the 'r' of 'rat' accounts for the cerebrals; the 'l' of 'love' positions the tongue for the dentals; and the position of tongue and lips to pronounce the 'w' of 'watch' is correct for the labial group.

1. The first group of consonants (guttural)

The first group uses the mouth position of the '*a*' for forming its five consonants so that this all takes place at the back of the mouth where it becomes the throat – the 'guttural' position.

a) k, k

The first consonant of this group is written '*k*', sounded 'ka' as in '*ka*rate'. An example of a commonly used Sanskrit term using this letter is '*karma*', literally meaning 'action'.

Clearly a consonant can occur at the end of the word, as with 'k' in 'rack' for example. Here, we do not want to sound an *a* with it. If we were to do so, we would end up with a different word – in this example it would become 'racka'. When this happens in Sanskrit an additional mark is added under the letter, called a *virAma*, literally meaning 'cessation', 'termination' or 'end', and is understood to mean 'don't make any vowel sound after this'. Consonants appearing at the end of a word, without a following vowel, are also called *halanta*. This means that a consonant, which for reasons I won't go into at the moment is represented by the abbreviation *hal*, is at the end, i.e. it is not followed by a vowel. Because of this, the *virAma* sign that indicates this is also called a *halant*. Thus, a *k* at the end of a word used to be written '*k.h*' in ITRANS, where the '.*h*' after any consonant means that it is followed by a halant and 'a' is not sounded after it. In fact, it is no longer necessary in ITRANS to do this – if the letter is written on its own at the end of a word, the halant is inserted automatically. The Devanagari letter for *k*, sounded 'ka' is:

क

And, when this appears at the end of a word and we do not want to sound the 'a' that is associated by default with the letter, a *halant* is added and it looks like:

क्

There is no corresponding mechanism in the Romanized transliteration scheme for differentiating between the two. It is simply assumed (as is the case now with ITRANS) that, if no vowel appears after a final consonant, then none is sounded. All of this is common sense really and it might be seen as an unnecessary complication. If you intend to go on to the second level, however, you will need to know why the form of a Devanagari character frequently looks slightly different when it appears at the end of a word.

b) kh, kh

The second consonant in the guttural group is written '*kh*'. Its pronunciation is much like the preceding one but with the addition of a slight breathy sound caused by actually letting out some air immediately following the 'k' sound. This method of uttering the sound is called 'aspirated'. It is often sounded like 'k-h' in 'cloa(k-h)at' but there is too much emphasis in this – it is really more subtle. Consonants such as '*k*' are said to be 'with little breath' (*alpaprANa*) while ones like '*kh*' are 'with much breath' (*mahAprANa*). Again, I am giving you the correct Sanskrit terms for these but I have not yet introduced all of the letters so you will not know precisely how to pronounce them. On the second and subsequent readings, of course, there will be no problem.

The word '*khaga*', meaning 'bird', is often used in textbooks teaching beginners of Sanskrit.

c) g, g

The third in this group is written '*g*', sounded '*g*' as in '*gap*' (sounded without any additional breath following the consonant, i.e. *alpaprANa*). A well-known word beginning with this letter is '*guru*', used to refer to a spiritual teacher, though its literal meaning is 'heavy'. In Sanskrit pronunciation, syllables that are emphasized (e.g. in reading poetry) are called *guru* as opposed to unstressed ones, which are called '*laghu*', meaning 'light'.

d) gh, gh

The fourth is written '*gh*' and, like '*kh*', is sounded with a super-seding expelling of air – *mahAprANa*. It sounds like '*gh*' in 'doghouse'. The word '*laghu*' just given above uses this consonant.

e) ~N, ṅ

The final consonant in this group introduces a new term – *anunAsika*, meaning that the sound is made through the nose as well as the throat. It is written using a tilde followed by a capital N in ITRANS format '~*N*' or with a dot above the lower case '*n*' in Romanized format. There are four n-related sounds; hence the need for the special characters. This one has the sound of '*ng*' made at the back of the throat and sounding through the nose, like 'sing' but with the ending further back in the throat like someone who is being strangled rather than singing!

The word ~Na itself means 'an object of sense' or 'desire for any sensual object', though, in the dictionary, it is designated as 'L', meaning 'lexicographers' rather than as a masculine, feminine or neuter noun. This means that no one has ever found the word being used in any scripture or other historical text.

2. The second group of consonants (palatal)

This second group forms the sounds in the back part of the mouth but not the throat. Based on the 'i' vowel, these use the back of the tongue and the rear of the mouth and are thus called 'palatal'. As noted above, a good guideline for this is to position the mouth and tongue for saying the y in 'yes'. They follow the same pattern as the previous group (as do all five of these groups of consonants, you will be pleased to know!). The first and third members are *alpaprANa*, the second and fourth are *mahAprANa*, and the fifth is *anunAsika*.

a) c or ch, c

The first is written 'c' or 'ch' in ITRANS and it is sounded like 'cha' in 'chap'. Whereas English pronounces this by using the *front* of the tongue near the *front* of the roof of the mouth, Sanskrit uses the *rear* parts.

It is likely that you are going to be confused over the choice of representations here when we look at the next letter in this group. ITRANS allows either of these forms to refer to the same letter, whereas Romanized transliteration insists on the first alone. It is perhaps understandable that 'ch' should be allowed since this is effectively how it sounds. There is no equivalent of the hard 'c' in English, as in 'tin can' – this would use the 'k' from the first group. Nor is there an equivalent of the soft 'c', as in 'cervix' – this would use the '*s*' that we will look at later. Therefore, there is actually no confusion in just using '*c*' to refer to this 'ch' sound. However, many sources do use *ch* and, since this is how it has to be sounded, I will use this form henceforth and *Ch* for the next letter.

An example that you will probably have encountered is '*chakra*'. It refers to the points in the spinal cord through which energy is supposed to flow and is particularly relevant in kundalini yoga.

b) chh or Ch, ch

The second character in this group used to be written '*chh*' in ITRANS but, unfortunately, '*ch*' in Romanized. More recently, ITRANS has introduced '*Ch*' as the preferred option, which avoids the confusion somewhat, so that it might be best for you to learn this from the outset and ignore the '*chh*' version altogether. Certainly, you need to decide which scheme you are using in any given document and stick to it!

Since I have already said that the pattern of the first group is repeated in the others, you might guess that this is sounded much like '*ch*' but with some added breath – and you would be right! Just remember not to make it too pronounced so that it comes out like 'mat(ch-h)ot' and it should be fine. If you are familiar with the Upanishads, you will know that one of the main ones is called the Chandogya. (Again this is not the correct transliterated spelling but the commonly used Anglicized one. I will always use normal font for these examples. If the font is italicized, you will know that it is the correct ITRANSliterated format.) The 'Ch' part of the word is this character.

c) j, j

The third is written '*j*' and pronounced more or less as we would expect, like the 'ja' in 'jam'. It uses minimum breath again as for all in this third 'row' of the main consonants. (The full table will be presented at the end of this section on the five main groups of consonants.) If you meditate using a mantra, you will probably know that the practice of mental repetition is called *japa*. This is a nice simple word pronounced exactly as you would expect, but remember to keep the vowels as short as possible – much shorter than typical English or American diction.

d) jh, jh

The fourth is written *jh* and you can work out now how it should sound – like 'j-ha' but not too much so. The frequency of letter occurrences in Sanskrit is very widely spread and there are quite a few letters that hardly occur at all. As noted above, the vowel *LLi* is very infrequent. (A longer version of it that will be discussed later is effectively non-existent!) *jh* is one of the less common consonants. An interesting example of a word that does use it emphasizes the need for care. In English there are words which, with just a slight variation in spelling, mean something quite different. Perhaps because there are so many more vowels in Sanskrit, this seems to happen much more often. The word *jhalA*, with a long 'a' sound at the end (which we have not yet discussed), means 'girl'. Spelling this with a short *a* at the end and two *l*'s gives *jhalla*, which means a 'prize-fighter'.

e) ~n (or JN), ñ

The final letter in this group is the second of the *anunAsika* characters (the 'n' type sounds made through the nose). It has a sort of 'ny' sound (as in 'canyon'). To pronounce this, put the tongue into the position in which you are about to say 'yes' and, without changing position, say 'nya'. This mouth movement is very alien to Westerners and, ideally, you should endeavor to listen to someone who knows how to pronounce the letter correctly. This applies to all of the letters but especially to ones such as this.

The only word listed in the dictionary beginning with this letter is another lexicographers' word, ~na, meaning a 'singer' or 'jingling sound' (or 'heretic' or 'ox'!). A common word that uses it, however, is j~nAna, as in jnana yoga, meaning 'knowledge'. This word is often confusingly represented in books, appearing sometimes as 'gyana' or 'gnana', and is very rarely pronounced correctly. This is not helped by the fact that the Itranslator Software permits *GY* to be used for the conjunct *j~n* so that *GYAna* is an allowable form of the ITRANS for this word. (The reason for this is that another transliteration scheme uses this form of representation – see Appendix 1.) The ITRANS *JN* is a more recent change, which is now recognized by the latest version of Itranslator software.

3. The third group of consonants (cerebral)

This third group has now moved the mouth position another step forward so that the roof of the mouth is used, with the tip of the tongue pointing up to it, as when you say 'rat'. To construct the main consonants, the tongue actually touches the roof. It is called the cerebral position.

a) T, ṭ

In ITRANS, all of this third (middle) group are written as capital letters to differentiate them from the fourth group, which appear very similar and also sound similar, simply moving the tongue nearer towards the front of the mouth. In the Romanized transliteration, the letters have a dot beneath them. '*T*' is pronounced as the 't' in 'tub', having the tongue pointing up to the roof of the palate as you say it. That should have been spoken 'with only a small breath' as usual (*alpaprANa*).

All of the letters in this group are infrequent. If you encounter a word with a sound that might be in this group, it is far more likely that it will in fact be in the next group. If your philosophy is that of Advaita, you are very likely to have heard of the sage Astavakra, born deformed because of a curse from his father while he was still in his mother's womb. (Astavakra means 'twisted in eight ways'.) The 'Astavakra Gita' records how he taught King Janaka the truths of Advaita. The 't' in Astavakra is actually this one.

b) Th, ṭh

The second letter is the aspirated form, sounded the same as '*T*' but with more breath as you make the sound (*mahAprANa*), a bit like 'po-<u>th</u>-ole' (pothole) – but remember that the tongue must point to the roof of the mouth, i.e. not how we would normally sound this combination.

c) D, ḍ

The next letter is pronounced like 'd' in 'dot' but as before, with the tip of the tongue right up in the roof of the mouth. Most spiritual seekers, whether or not they belong to the Advaita school, will have heard of the philosopher Adi Shankara, who systematized the philosophy of Advaita in the eighth century AD. The teacher of Shankara's teacher was Gaudapada, who is famous for writing a verse-commentary (*kArikA*) on one of the Upanishads – the Mandukya Upanishad. Unfortunately, all of these Sanskrit words are incorrectly represented, as you will discover later. But, for the moment, we can improve on this situation by acknowledging that the first 'd' in 'Gaudapada' and the one in 'Mandukya' are in fact this character, '*D*' – the cerebral form of the 'd' sounding letter.

d) Dh, ḍh

The fourth letter sounds the same as the third but with more breath (e.g. go-dh-ead). An example is *Dhola*, which is a large drum.

e) N, ṇ

The last in the group is another 'na' sound but with the tongue in the roof of the mouth. The word *guNa* uses this letter – and here is the first complete word consisting completely of letters you have now met. Instead of writing it (incorrectly) as 'guna', you can now use the correct transliteration of *guNa* or **guṇa**. It refers to the three 'qualities' of nature in Sankhya yoga – *sattva*, *rajas* and *tamas*.

4. The fourth group of consonants (dental)

This group of consonants is sounded with the tongue positioned just behind the teeth, as though to say 'love', and called, unsurprisingly, dental. The sounds are essentially the same as those in the cerebral group but sound much more natural to Western ears and are very much more common. If you are ever in any doubt as to whether a sound should be cerebral or dental, guess this one!

a) t, t

The first member of the group is '*t*'. It is sounded with the tongue actually touching the back of the teeth. This is further forward in the mouth than is normally used in English and is better represented by a word such as the French 'petite'. A simple example, or even two examples, is *tat* as in the *mahAvAkya* ('great saying' from the Upanishads) *tat tvam asi* – 'thou art that'. It means 'that' and both t's are this dental character (in fact, this word begins its life as *tad*, as you will discover later). The final 't' is the *halanta* form, meaning that there is no vowel sound following it and the Devanagari character will have a halant sign beneath it, whereas the first one will not.

b) th, th

Then comes the equivalent aspirated letter, with more breath (*mahAprANa*), '*th*', pronounced as in 'butthead'. (Another way in which this letter is pronounced – and those who do so would maintain it to be the correct way! – is as the English 'th' in 'path', for example. It has to be said that it seems easier, and more consistent, to pronounce the word *sthita*, for example, as is indicated in the main text.) The adjective *sthita* means 'standing' and is used in the sense of 'steady' and 'firm' in the word *sthitapraj~na* in the Bhagavad Gita, where it means 'a person of steady wisdom' or someone who knows the Self.

c) d, d

Next is '*d*'. This is essentially the same as in 'dog' but with the tongue starting out immediately behind the teeth. Perhaps the French 'donner' might be a better representation. The word *dama* means 'self-restraint', understood as control over the senses. It is one of the six qualities specified by Shankara as prerequisites for the spiritual seeker.

d) dh, dh

This is the breathy equivalent of the previous character and is pronounced as the 'dh' in 'adhere'. A similar word to *dama*, as just described, is *dharma*. This word is possibly more familiar to many readers. It is commonly used to speak of such things as recommended practice, duty or conduct, and to refer to absolutes of justice etc. More appropriately, in a spiritual context, it means essence or essential quality or nature. Our own *dharma* refers to what we ought to be doing with our lives in order to move forward on some path towards realization of our Self.

e) n, n

Finally, in this group, is the one sounded through the nose (*anunAsika*). This is pronounced just as in English, as for example in… er… 'nose'. The word *nAma* is a simple word, meaning 'name', as in the phrase *nAma-rUpa*, the 'name and form' of the creation that is, in reality, non-dual, not separate from ourselves and not actually created, according to Advaita.

Quite often the 'n' at the end of a word will be replaced by the nasal in the same group as the consonant that follows. This is because the rules that govern how letters combine are designed so that sound flows smoothly without gaps or stutters. It would be extremely difficult to make the correct sound of one of these *anunAsika* consonants, immediately followed by the correct sound of another consonant, unless the two are in the same group – try it later!

Thus, an example of a word with which you are likely to be familiar, and which uses this letter, is 'satsa~Nga'. This would typically be written as 'satsang' in books for the Western market. It refers to the 'good company' of associating with like-minded people, and especially with ones who are Self-realized. It is used for the question-and-answer sessions provided by the teachers who currently tour the Western world. The *anunAsika* used has to be '~N' because it is combined with the immediately following 'g' and, since this is in the first, guttural, group of consonants, so must the nasal letter be.

5. The fifth group of consonants (labial)

The final group of the main consonants is sounded at the lips. They are called 'labial' and pronounced with the lips in the position as if to say 'woo' (or, as some say, as if to kiss a baby).

a) p, p

The first is '*p*' just like our 'p', as in 'put'. The theory of *karma* tells us that we are effectively 'rewarded' as a result of 'good' or unselfish acts and 'punished' by 'bad' or selfish ones, if not in this life, then in future ones. The result of good action is called *puNya*; the result of bad action is called *pApa*. Both begin with this labial character.

b) ph, ph

Then comes the corresponding breathy '*ph*', as in uphill. In respect of the karma just mentioned, books will often speak of the 'fruit' of action being either good or bad. The Sanskrit for 'fruit' is *phalam*, beginning with this letter, and 'fruit of action' is *karmaphalam*. You have to remember not to pronounce this as 'falam', thinking that the 'ph' sound is the same as in English!

c) b, b

Next is '*b*', as in 'bad'. *buddha* means 'awake' or 'enlightened'. (Note that this word also contains both *d* and *dh* from the dental group, in a compound consonant.)

d) bh, bh

The *mahAprANa* '*bh*' is pronounced as in 'abhor'. The Bhagavad Gita begins with this letter. *bhagavat* means 'prosperous, happy'.

gItA, when correctly spelt, does not in fact contain short vowels but long ones, which we will look at in just a moment – it means 'sung'. A *gItA* is usually a philosophical or religious doctrine in the form of a sacred song or poem. Note that the '*t*' at the end of *bhagavat* becomes a '*d*' when it joins with *gItA* to become *bhagavadgItA*.

e) m, m

Finally, the *anunAsika* in this group is '*m*', pronounced as in 'man'. An example of its use is the word *manas*, which strictly speaking means 'mind' in its widest sense, including intellect, understanding, perception, conscience etc. In Hindu philosophies in particular though, it is used in a much more specific sense. It refers to that part of the mind responsible for transmitting information from the senses to the part responsible for discrimination and judgment (*buddhi*) and then sending instructions back again to the arms and legs etc. Unfortunately, *manas* tends not to restrict itself to these proper functions but gets involved in 'thinking' – and this is the cause of many of our problems!

6. Table of basic consonants

The table of the five groups of consonants, with the corresponding vowel shown in Column 1 for reference, is as shown below:

Table 1 – The Basic Consonants

Guttural	*a, a*	k, k	kh, kh	g, g	gh, gh	~N, ṅ
Palatal	*i, i*	ch, c	Ch, ch	j, j	jh, jh	~n, ñ
Cerebral	*RRi, ṛ*	T, ṭ	Th, ṭh	D, ḍ	Dh, ḍh	N, ṇ
Dental	*LLi, ḷ*	t, t	th, th	d, d	dh, dh	n, n
Labial	*u, u*	p, p	ph, ph	b, b	bh, bh	m, m

This table will be expanded later to show the entire alphabet.

C. The Long Vowels

The five simple vowels that we looked at above are all *short* vowels – *hrasva*. This means that, when pronounced, the sound is made as short as possible while still being distinguishable – quite short! Each of these vowels can be sounded long and each long form is treated as effectively a separate vowel. The duration of the spoken sound is very precise. If the short form is treated as one measure, then the long form should be two measures. (A measure is called a *mAtrA* in Sanskrit.) The long form is called *dIrgha* and the '*I*' here is an example of the *dIrgha* form of '*i*'. In ITRANS, the vowel is shown as long either by putting two of them, as in *diirgha*, or by capitalizing it thus: *dIrgha*. In Romanized transliteration, the long form is represented by a macron above the letter, i.e. *ī* in this example. To maintain the format of the presentation, we will look at each vowel in turn, giving an example.

1. aa or A, ā

When the vowels become long, the pronunciation naturally changes slightly, too. Thus, the short '*a*' becomes '*aa*' or '*A*' and sounds like the 'a' in 'car'. The difference between short and long vowels can be appreciated by comparing 'cut' and 'car'. The word *Atman*, referring to one's true nature, the Self, which in Advaita is the same as the universal Self, *brahman*, begins with a long 'A', while the second 'a' in the word is short.

2. ii or I, ī

The short '*i*' becomes '*ii*' or '*I*' and sounds like the double 'ee' sound in words like 'beet'. The difference between short and long vowels can be appreciated by comparing 'bit' and 'beet'. The *gItA*, meaning 'sung', has already been mentioned. It is a common abbreviation for the *bhagavadgItA*, though there is also the other famous Advaita text – the Astavakra Gita. (The correct transliteration of this would be *aShTAvakra gItA* but we have not yet encountered some of the other letters.)

3. R^I or RRI, r̄

The short '*R^i*' or '*RRi*' becomes '*R^I*' or 'RRI'. Here there is no option of having two small i's. The Romanized version follows the same rule as for the other vowels, simply adding a macron. The *dIrgha* vowel is sounded as for the *hrasva* but with an 'ee' ending instead of 'i'. This vowel normally only occurs in the endings of some parts of some nouns and since this book is not addressing grammatical aspects, we can safely ignore it.

4. L^I or LLI, l̄

Similarly, the short '*L^i*' or '*LLi*' becomes '*L^I*' or 'LLI' but, since there are no words at all known to contain it, this hardly seems to matter! Its existence seems merely to satisfy the need for logical completeness.

5. uu or U, ū

Finally, short '*u*' becomes long '*uu*' or '*U*' and sounds like the double 'oo' in 'root'. The difference between short and long vowels can be appreciated by comparing 'put' and 'root'. The word *sUtra* uses the long form. It literally means a 'thread' or 'string'. It is usually used to refer to the terse verse-form used in scriptures to formulate the essence of some philosophical thought. Here the sense is of a thread that holds everything together like the beads of a necklace. Note that verses in the Vedas are usually referred to as *mantra*-s, since they are often used as objects of meditation. You should also note here the practice of adding an English '-s' to a Sanskrit word to make it into a plural. This is to avoid having to learn the endings of nouns, which would depend on declension, gender and number. Here, for example, the correct plural of *sUtra* should be *sUtrANi*.

6. The even longer vowels

The vowels can be sounded for longer than two measures, in which case they are called *pluta*, meaning 'prolonged'. In this case, they are written with a number '3' below and just to the right of the letter, both in Devanagari and in the Romanized version: '*a₃*'. a3 in ITRANS generates the Devanagari character with a (Devanagari) 3 adjacent to it rather than as a subscript. Having noted its existence, you really do not have to remember it; it is not usually encountered in words, being more relevant to chanting etc.

The well-known Sanskrit word 'OM' does employ a *pluta* sound for the 'o' but ITRANS uses the capital letters shown (OM) for this character and not the number 3.

One use of the prolonged vowel is similar to the corresponding usage in English, namely when calling someone from a distance. When *rAma* is down the road and we want to catch his attention we might call 'rAAAAAmaaaaa!' or *ra3ma3*.

D. The Complex Vowels and Additional Sounds

We have not quite finished with vowels yet, as you will probably have realized, if you are at all familiar with Sanskrit terms. There are four vowels that result from combining the sounds of the three simple vowels: *a*, *i* and *u*. In some grammar books you will see them referred to as diphthongs.

1. e, e

When *a* is allowed to continue sounding beyond its natural, short measure, you get the prolonged '*a₃*' sound. If this is allowed to continue sounding and you then raise the back of the tongue towards the '*i*' position, but stop before you get there, you should hear the sound of the first compound vowel, '*e*'. It's a bit like the 'a' in 'mate' but not so open as speakers of British English would usually pronounce this. '*e*' can be regarded as the combination of '*a*' and '*i*'. It is sounded with the *dīrgha* measure, as are all of these four compound vowels, since they are effectively two vowel-sounds combined. It occurs in the word *deva*, meaning 'god' and, no, we haven't yet met that 'v' character!

2. ai, ai

If, after making the above sound for '*e*', you relax the tongue back towards the '*a*' position but again stop before you get there, there is another sound formed as a compound between '*a*' and '*e*'. It sounds like the 'ie' in 'pie'. It is written '*ai*' and it occurs in the dualistic philosophy *dvaita*, and of course the non-dualistic one *advaita*. The letter '*a*' in front of a word always negates it. Thus, *vidya* means 'knowledge' and *avidya* means 'ignorance'. ('v' and 'y' will be dealt with in the very next section.)

3. o, o

If the sound '*a*' is made and allowed to continue to sound while the mouth is slowly closed, the sound made before the lips come together is '*u*'. If these two sounds are made together or, more practically speaking, if the sound corresponding to the mid-point between these two is made, the sound that emerges is '*o*' (as in 'boat'). Since you are reading this book, you are presumably a spiritual seeker and your aim in life is therefore Self-realization, enlightenment or liberation. The Sanskrit for 'liberation' is *mokSha*.

4. au, au

In a similar way to that described above for *ai*, if the mouth moves from the '*a*' (open-mouthed) position to the '*o*' (partially closed) position but stops halfway, there is a sound similar to 'ow' in 'town'. This is written '*au*' in ITRANS. Gaudapada was mentioned above as being the author of the Mandukya Upanishad but I did not give the full transcription. Since we have now covered all of the letters in his name, here it is – *gauDapAda*, giving an example of this compound vowel as well as a long and short 'a' and the two types of 'd'.

5. M or .n, ṃ or ṁ

All of the 14 vowels have now been covered but there are two final letters to bc added to complete the group of 16 so-called *mAtRRikA* (literally meaning 'divine mothers' but used in the sense of written characters that have magical powers. The 16 vowels are also sometimes called *shakti*, which also means 'power' or 'strength'.) These are not really vowels themselves but act as modifications to a preceding vowel. Note that, because of this, if they are talked about as letters in their own right, they assume an 'a' before rather than after.

The first of these is called an *anusvAra*, meaning 'after sound', and is represented in Devanagari by a dot positioned above the preceding vowel. It is written as '*M*' or '*.n*' and is sounded through the nose alone (whereas the other nasal sounds are made with nose and throat). In Romanized methods, it may be represented with a dot either above or below the 'm'. The best-known Sanskrit–English dictionary, by Monier-Williams, uses the 'below' variant, while the Itranslator software mentioned later uses the 'above' variant.

The 'overdot' is produced in ITRANS by either *M* or *.n* but the latter should be used when the symbol is required in the middle of a word and the following letter is a consonant other than a labial one, where the former should be used. This helps us remember to sound it with the correct nasal. I will normally use *M* in all cases, however, since the dictionary software utility which I will tell you about later, for example, does not recognize the *.n* construction.

The *anusvAra* is not a letter in its own right but a replacement for the letter *m* at the end of a word or in special cases for *m* or *n* in the middle of a compound. For the sake of euphonic harmony (called *saMdhi*, and discussed later) the *anusvAra* is replaced by the nasal of the family of the consonant that follows it. So the *anusvAra* at the end of a word will change to ~*N* if the word following begins with a guttural letter, to ~*n* if followed by a word beginning with a palatal letter, *N* if followed by a word starting with a cerebral letter, etc. There are three letters that do not require a change in the *anusvAra*: *sh*, *Sh* and *s*. If these follow, the *anusvAra* remains in the form of an *anusvAra* and is sounded through the nose only.

An example with which you will almost certainly be familiar is *saMsAra*, referring to the 'eternal round' of birth and death that we apparently endure in the phenomenal world.

6. H, ḥ

The other special letter that is not really part of the alphabet is called a '*visarga*', which means a 'sending out', 'emission' etc. It is represented by two dots (like a colon) placed to the right of the associated letter in Devanagari script. It is written '*H*' and it has the effect of adding a brief, breathing out, 'unvoiced' sound after the vowel.

The *visarga* is a replacement for the letter 's' at the end of a word and is often changed to another letter depending on what precedes or follows. In particular, you will find a *visarga* at the end of a sentence or before the letters *sh*, *Sh*, *s* as well as *k*, *kh*, *p*, *ph*. In a number of traditions the *visarga* is sounded as an echo of the vowel that precedes it so *rAmaH* will be pronounced 'rAmaha', *hariH* as 'harihi', *guruH* as 'guruhu etc. Before a *p* or *ph*, it takes on the sound of a gentle 'f' so that *pUrNamadaH pUrNamidam* is sounded 'pUrNamada-f-pUrNamidam'. Before *k* or *kh* it takes on a sound a bit like hissing or gently clearing the throat.

The Sanskrit for the overall 'organ' of mind, referring to the seat of thought and feeling, is called *antaHkaraNa*. It consists of the intellect (*buddhi*), responsible for discrimination and judgment; the memory (*chitta*); the function (*manas*) responsible for transmitting information from the senses and back to the organs of action; and the ego (*aha~NkAra*).

So, to recap, the 16 *mAtRRikA* are as follows:

Table 2 – The 16 *mAtRRikA*

a	aa	i	ii	u	uu	RRi	RRI	LLI	e	o	ai	au	aM	aH
	or		or		or									
	A		I		U									

E. The Semi-Vowels

There are two small groups of consonants left. The first of these is the group of four so-called 'semi-vowels' or *antaHstha*. They are formed by combining the sound of each of the four main vowels other than 'a' with the sound of 'a' itself. Each should be sounded at the appropriate mouth position, corresponding to the vowel that forms its starting point.

1. y, y

If you sound '*i*' and then immediately change the mouth position to that of the '*a*' sound while still making the sound, what emerges sounds like 'ya' and this is the first semi-vowel: '*y*' as in 'yes'. This is the semi-vowel at the palatal position. There is none at the guttural position since this is the position of 'a' itself. Everyone will know the word *yoga*, even if not spiritually inclined.

2. r, r

If you sound the vowel '*RRi*' in the cerebral position, with the tongue towards the roof of the mouth, and combine it with the '*a*' sound, you get '*r*' as in 'rat'. *rajas* is the second of the three *guNa*; the quality associated with activity and passion.

3. l, l

If you sound the vowel '*LLi*' in the dental position and combine it with the '*a*' sound, you get '*l*' as in 'love'. The idea of God's creating the universe in order to 'play' or 'amuse' himself is called *lIlA* – two 'l' semi-vowels together with *dIrgha* versions of 'i' and 'a'.

4. v, v

Finally, if you sound '*u*' in the labial position and combine this with an '*a*', you get '*v*', which is sounded as the 'w' in 'wag'. Note that Americans seem to prefer to ignore this logical derivation and pronounce it as 'va' in 'van'. But then it is also somewhat illogical to write it as 'v' while sounding it as 'w'. I must confess that, having started out pronouncing it correctly, I now usually pronounce it as 'v', since most people don't understand you otherwise. (Not that most understand anyway!)

The word *vedAnta*, often written with a capital 'V', literally means 'end' or 'culmination' (*anta*) of the Vedas, since that is where most of the Upanishads will be found. The four Vedas are the documents that form the essence of Hindu philosophy. The first part of the Vedas – called *karmakANDa* – relates to ritualistic teachings, which are given primacy by *pUrvamimAmsa* philosophy. The last part is called *j~nAnakANDa* and it is this that brings enlightenment according to Advaita. *veda* itself actually means 'knowledge' but it is not really correct to say that *vedAnta* means 'end of knowledge'. The four Vedas are the documents that form the essence of Hindu philosophy.

F. The Sibilants

Almost last of all in the Sanskrit alphabet are three sibilants or sss-sounds. A sibilant is called *UShman* in Sanskrit, and the 'Sh' in the middle of this word is the second of these three letters. They are in the palatal, cerebral and dental positions, respectively. In theory, there are also ones in the other two positions but these are so rare that they are invariably ignored.

1. sh, ś

In the palatal position, there is '*sh*' sounded by making a shh sound in that mouth position. It sounds like the 'sh' in 'cash'. I have just mentioned the Vedas as being the main source for Hindu philosophies. These are often referred to as *shruti*, which literally means 'hearing' and refers to the fact that they are essentially orally transmitted wisdom, passed on from generation to generation.

2. shh or Sh, ṣ

The second, in the cerebral position, is '*shh*' or '*Sh*', similar to the 'sh' sound in 'shall' but with the tongue up to the roof of the mouth. Continuing the theme of the Vedas, these '*shruti*' are said to be '*apauruSheya*', using this second sibilant in the middle of the word. This literally means 'not coming from human beings' but is usually translated as 'unauthored'.

3. s, s

Finally, there is the dental '*s*', sounding like the normal 's' in 'sand'. The spiritual disciplines that we follow in search of our goal of Self-realization are called *sAdhana*. This means 'leading straight to a goal' and is used to talk about any sort of spiritual path in this sense.

G. h, h

This brings us to the last letter in the alphabet, *h*, sounding as you would expect, as 'h' in 'hat'. It is sometimes considered another sibilant and is also called *UShman*, which literally means 'heated'. The word '*aham*', meaning 'I', uses this letter. Note that in most Anglicized words where an 'h' appears *after* another consonant, such as dharma, Shankara, chakra, Katha Upanishad, there will not be a letter 'h' present in the Sanskrit word. In these examples, the actual letters are '*dh*' in *dharma*, '*sh*' in *sha~Nkara*, '*ch*' in *chakra* and '*th*' in *katha*. It is in those words where the 'h' appears, either on its own as in *aham* or *before* another consonant, as in *brahma*, that it really will be a '*h*'.

It should be noted that this letter also has characteristics of the semi-vowels and is sometimes listed with those rather than with the sibilants. You will see later that, in the *shivasUtrANi*, it is actually grouped with the semi-vowels: *ha-ya-va-ra-T*.

H. The Complete Alphabet

The order of the alphabet, if you want to look up a word in the dictionary, is as follows. The 16 *mAtRRikA* are at the beginning, in the order as shown in Table 2 earlier. Next come the five main groups of consonants, in the order guttural, palatal, cerebral, dental and labial. Then come the four semi-vowels, the three sibilants and finally *h*, 49 characters in total. Table 3 summarizes the alphabet in columns of similar sounds.

Table 3 – The Complete Alphabet

A	*e*	*ai*	*I*	*RRI*	*LLI*	*U*	*o*	*au*		
a			*i*	*RRi*	*LLi*	*u*			*M*	*H*
k			*ch*	*T*	*t*	*p*				
kh			*Ch*	*Th*	*th*	*ph*				
g			*j*	*D*	*d*	*b*				
gh			*jh*	*Dh*	*dh*	*bh*				
~N			*~n*	*N*	*n*	*m*				
			y	*r*	*l*	*v*				
h			*sh*	*Sh*	*s*					

The '*a*' sounds, made almost in the throat, are called 'guttural' or *kaNThya*. The '*i*' sounds, made a little further forward using the hard palate, are called 'palatal' or *tAlavya*. The '*RRI*' sounds have the tongue beginning near the roof of the mouth and are called 'cerebral' or *mUrdhanya*. The '*LLI*' sounds are made behind the upper front teeth and are called 'dental' or *dantya*. The '*u*' sounds are made with the lips pouting in a small circle and are called 'labial' or *oShThya*.

Level 2 The Devanagari Script

This level will now repeat the previous material but introduce each of the Sanskrit letters in the correct Devanagari script. We will also look at some of the ways in which letter forms vary depending on their position in the word and upon the nature of any adjacent letters.

A. The Five Basic (Simple) Vowels, Short and Long

1. a, a; aa or A, ā

(The heading here is the format that I will use for each letter in this level. It should be understood as: **a** in ITRANS, **a** in Roman; **aa or A** in ITRANS, ā in Roman)

The Devanagari form of this letter was shown earlier, the only one that we have met so far. When it appears at the beginning of a word or when being written as a 'stand-alone' letter, it is written as follows:

अ

This is the simple, short (*hrasva*) form. The long (*dīrgha*) form looks very similar:

आ

You will probably have seen Sanskrit script at some time. If not, it would be surprising that you are reading this book. This being the case, you will have realized that, when characters are joined together to make a word, there is a continuous line at the top of the word spanning all of the characters. If you have looked at the scriptures, you may have thought that some of the words are exceedingly long! In fact, words are frequently joined together, depending on the nature of the sounds ending one word and beginning the next. Also, many words are formed as compounds, similar to those in the German language. In Sanskrit, this is called *samAsa* and can result in very long words that are effectively a mixture of nouns and adjectives.

Written Sanskrit is very efficient in its use of space and 'shorthand' is frequently used. Accordingly, in the *dIrgha* form of *a* here, all that is done is to add an extra downstroke to the *hrasva* form and extend the bar at the top. Thus, you can see that the *hrasva* form has a single downstroke and the *dIrgha* form has two downstrokes.

It has already been noted that all consonants, when sounded on their own, are sounded with the vowel '*a*' by convention. In fact when writing the consonant '*m*' it is strictly written as follows (with the *halanta* stroke beneath):

म्

This cannot be pronounced until the letter *a* (or any other vowel) is added. The effect of this is for the *halanta* sign to be removed. So *ma* looks like this:

म

Thus, the word *maha*, for example, meaning 'great', 'strong', 'abundant' etc., is made up of the letters *m* + *a* + *h* + *a*.

म् + अ + ह + अ

It is the word that forms part of *maharShi* in Ramana Maharshi, for example. Here, *maharShi* means *maha RRiShi* or 'great sage or saint'. The letters in *maha* will be sounded *ma* and *ha*.

The character for *ma* is: म

and that for *ha* is: ह

so that the word *maha* is written: मह

Another letter ahead of its place in the development is *y* or *ya*. This is written:

यू or य

To return to the discussion of *a*, we can now see the use of the extra downstroke to lengthen the vowel in the word *mAyA*. This is usually just written 'maya' in Anglicized texts. It refers to the force that is supposedly wielded by Ishvara to create the universe. The Devanagari representation is:

माया

which should be understood as consisting of:

म् + आ + यू + आ

The single downstroke following a consonant (or a combination of consonants) means that it/they is/are sounded with *A*, instead of just *a*. Appendix 3 looks at each of the vowels and how a consonant changes when used with them.

Before moving on, it must be mentioned that the principal Sanskrit–English dictionary, by M. Monier-Williams, uses a rather different version of this character. It is unfortunate that the very first letter to be encountered should occur in variants but it is as well that you be warned that this does occur for a few letters, though this does not usually cause any problems. This alternative character for '*a*' looks like this:

अ

And it adds a second vertical line at the right in just the same way when made into the *dīrgha* vowel. Appendix 2 lists those letters that may be found using alternative forms to those used in this book and shows these different forms for comparison. In the main text, I will only show variants where these are found in Monier-Williams, since this is a likely reference for readers. The other source of variants is the School of Economic Science in England. They do have a few variations on the letter forms most commonly used elsewhere.

2. i, i; ii or I, ī

The Devanagari form of the *hrasva* form of this character is:

इ = *i* and the *dīrgha* form is ई = *ii* or *I*.

The short form is like the letter 's' hanging from the top bar, with a curl in its tail. For lengthening the vowel, a 'hook' shape, open to the right, is added to the top of the letter. It is this element that is taken and modified in order to represent the use of this letter when it combines with a consonant. An example of the short *i* in a word is *milita*, meaning 'met, encountered' or 'connected, combined with'.

In combination with a consonant, short *i* – इ – is written as ि and placed *in front of* the consonant.

Thus, *milita* is written:

मिलित

The three consonants in this word – *m*, *l*, and *t* – will be encountered later.

The significant point to glean from this example is the representation of *mi* and *li*. What is done is to put a vertical line *before* the consonant, and then join the top of the line to the top of the consonant by a 'hook' form similar to that which distinguishes the long vowel on its own.

There might be some concern at the apparent reversal of the symbols here – the symbol of *i* being written before the symbols of *m* and *l* – so that the *mi* and *li* appear to be read from right to left, as it were. The simple explanation for this is that we need to distinguish the short *i* from the long *I* in combination.

In combination ई is written as ी and placed *after* the consonant.

The word *jIva* is used to refer to what is often called the 'embodied Self', the mistaken identification of our true nature with a limited body and mind.

जीव

The letter *j* is obviously ज्

After this is added an extra vertical line which is then joined back to the top of the *j*. Since the *j* is now sounded with a vowel, the halant sign is dropped. The letter व is a simple (*halanta*) *v* joined to a short *a*.

3. R^i or RRi, ṛ; R^I or RRI, ṝ

The Devanagari forms of the *hrasva* and *pluta* versions of this letter are:

ऋ – *RRi*; ॠ – *RRI*

Here, the key part to remember is the 'hook' (or double-hook for the *dIrgha* form) hanging down at the right of the letter. It is this part alone that is used when the vowel appears in combination with a consonant. Thus, if the vowel is attached to the consonant *k* to become *kRRi*, for example, the Devanagari form changes as below:

क् changes to कृ

i.e. a simple hook is added to the bottom of the vertical line of the main character, *k* (and the *halanta* symbol dropped). The word *kRRita* means 'done', 'performed', 'made ready' etc. and is written:

कृत

The letter *t* – त्– appears with *a* following (and its *halanta* sign dropped), while the 'hook' at the bottom of the *k* indicates that it is sounded with *RRi*.

It would be useful to add a warning here, incidentally. The vowel *RRi* must not be confused with the semi-vowel *r*. There is a word *kriyA* for example, which means 'doing', 'performing' etc. It has no *RRi* vowel present at all but uses the consonant *k* and semi-vowel *r* together with the vowel *i*. If ever in any doubt, this latter form is the more likely. Remember that the vowel *RRi* is not very common, *RRI* is even less common, *LLi* is hardly ever seen and *LLI* is never seen.

4. LLi or L^i, ऌ ; LLI or L^I, ॡ

The Devanagari forms of the *hrasva* and *dIrgha* versions of this letter are:

ऌ and ॡ

but, given what has been said above, I will not provide any examples. It is sufficient to say that, in the unlikely event of these vowels appearing in combination with a consonant, the entire letter is used beneath the consonant. Thus, in combination with the letter *k*, for example:

क् – *k* becomes कॢ – *kLLi*

5. u, u; uu or U, ū

The Devanagari form of the *hrasva* form is:

उ and the *dIrgha* form is: ऊ

Here is another way of modifying the basic letter form to signify a different vowel sound. When it comes to using this vowel in the middle of a word, following a consonant, again we do not use the letter itself but a shorthand version. The short *u* sound is represented by a '9' shape, lying on its back, as it were, beneath the preceding consonant. If it is a long *U* sound, then the shape is inverted.

I will use the word *guru* as an illustration here because you will have to find out eventually that the letter *r* does not always behave itself and follow the rules. In the case of sounding with *u* (and *U*), instead of adding the symbol beneath the letter like all of the other consonants, it forms its own specially modified symbol. Thus, the *gu* part of the word is as expected.

The letter *g* looks like: ग्as a pure consonant
and गु if combined with *u*.
The letter *r* is written र् as a pure consonant
but रु with a *u*.
Thus the word *guru* is written: गुरु

The classical five gross elements (ether, air, fire, water, earth) are called the *mahAbhUtAni* (plural), with any one of them being a *mahAbhUta*. The Devanagari for this is:

महाभूत

with the '9' shape lying 'face down' underneath the *bh* character,

भू

It is worth noting at this point the similarity of the symbol for *halanta* and the symbol for long *'U'*. The former doesn't have a curl – ◌ – whereas the latter has: ◌

So make a note of the distinction between the pure consonant म्

and the *bh* combined with long *U* – मू – in which the *halanta* sign is dropped and replaced by the symbol for *U*.

B. The Five Main Groups of Consonants

The Sanskrit term for consonants is *vya~njana*. One of the meanings of this is simply 'a consonant' but it also has the sense of an 'indication' or a 'decoration' (of the basic vowel sound). They are formed by positioning the mouth (throat, tongue or lips) in such a way as to 'stop' or modify the sound of the vowel in various ways. These are called the 'outer efforts'. There are more subtle changes to the body involved in modifying the vowel. These are the 'inner efforts'. To be able to discern the difference requires very fine observation of the changes to the body. Try this experiment:

Shut your eyes and get poised to make the sound *ka*. Without making even the slightest sound, note the slightly pinched state of the throat; note how the tongue lies flat but is also tensed in anticipation. Now observe the slight tension between the eyebrows and forehead, and also observe what's happening in the areas of the chest and belly – how they are tensed in preparation for making the sound.

Relax, breathe out...

Now, without making a sound, change the set-up as though to make the sound *ga*. Note the comparative relaxation of forehead and tongue. Note how the bottom of the throat and chest seem to come into play and the belly relaxes.

Relax, breathe out...

Go from *ka* to *ga* in this way until you are clear about what is different.

The very set-up *is* the consonant. Looked at this way, we understand the consonant to be merely the bodily condition through which we sound the vowels. The consonant has no sound of its own. That's why it should strictly be written with the *halanta* or *virAma* symbol. Without this symbol, we know that the short '*a*' has been added so that the consonant can manifest.

1. The guttural or *kaNThya* consonants

The first group uses the same mouth position as *a* and takes place at the back of the mouth where it becomes the throat – the 'guttural' or *kaNThya* – position.

a) k, k

The first consonant of this group is written:

क् (or क when a is added) – An example is *kAma*, meaning 'desire' or 'longing': काम (Note the extra vertical line for the long *A*.)

Although it cannot be sounded on its own without a vowel, it could occur at the end of the word (as 'k' in 'rack' for example). In this case, it would have the *virAma* sign after it. This looks like:

क् – The verb *lak* means to 'taste' or 'obtain': लक्

This use of the *virAma* applies to all consonants. Note, incidentally, that it is the form of the letter + *a* that is used for a consonant being pronounced when sounding the alphabet – this is by convention only and has no other significance. From here on we will write the letters with the 'a' added (and the *halanta* sign dropped).

b) kh, kh

The second consonant in the *kaNThya* group is the *mahAprANa* 'k' sound, written:

ख

An example of its use is given in connection with the next letter.

c) g, g

The third in this group is written:

ग

The word *khaga* was given as an example of *kh* in Level 1. It means 'moving in air', or more specifically, 'bird':

खग

Strictly speaking, when referring to nouns, account ought to be taken of the fact that Sanskrit nouns have gender. *khaga* is in fact masculine and would be written *khagaH* in the nominative case, with a *visarga* (see Level 1 Section D 6):

खगः

It has to be recognized that Sanskrit is similar to languages such as Latin, in the sense that nouns change their endings according to the part of speech being played in the sentence. Verbs, too, conjugate in a similar way with endings dependent upon tense and number (which can be 'one', 'two' or 'more than two'). But I will not be addressing any of these aspects in this book.

d) gh, gh

The fourth guttural consonant is written:

घ

We have already met the word *laghu*, meaning 'light' or 'short' (and the opposite of the more frequently encountered *guru*). It is written:

लघु

e) ~N, ṅ

The final consonant in this group is the nasal, *anunAsika*, ~*N*, and it is written:

ङ

The word that is used to give a name to the way in which our true Self becomes identified with something (object or idea) in the outside world is usually written 'ahankara' in Anglicized texts. It is often used interchangeably with our word 'ego'. In fact it derives from two words – *aham* meaning 'I' and *kAra* meaning 'doer' – the effective interpretation being 'I am the doer'.

Now you will see if you look at some Sanskrit sentences that many of the words seem very long. This is because individual small words, adjacent to each other in a sentence, are combined together unless a spoken syllable naturally coincides with the end of a word. Also, there are a number of rules governing the way in which various sounds combine when they appear next to each other. These prevent, for example, the situation where one word ends in a vowel and the next word begins with one, by merging the two. For example, if the first ends in *a* or *A* and the next begins with *a* or *A* then the two words are joined with just one *A*. These rules are comprehensive and logical so that the sorts of problems encountered in other languages are avoided. I will mention a few of these rules later.

Accordingly, in this example, when *aham* and *kAra* come together, it would not sound natural to make the 'm' sound and immediately follow it with a 'k'. The Sanskrit *k* is sounded at the back of the throat and it sounds far more natural to sound the *kaNThya ~N* since it is the same position. Try sounding them both and see. The resulting sound of the two consonants combined is similar to the Egyptian 'ankh' sounded at the back of the throat. So the resulting word is sounded *aha~NkAra*. In fact, the Devanagari script is not usually written to reflect this, even though it is, strictly speaking, the correct representation. This is because of the *anusvAra* that was dealt with in Level 1 Section D 5. This is often used in the middle of a word whenever we want to make an *anunAsika* consonant whose precise sound will depend upon the consonant that follows. And regardless of this sound, it can always be represented by the dot placed above the preceding consonant. Devanagari is very economical! Thus, this word appears as *ahaMkAra*. (ITRANS allows you to represent this instead as *aha.nkAra*. This generates exactly the same Devanagari but reminds us that this is an internal *anunAsika* followed by a consonant which is not a labial.)

अहंकार

The first letter is *a* – अ

which this time appears in its full glory since it is the first letter in the word.

The next letter is *h*, briefly met earlier – हॖ

followed by अ giving us ह

Next we have मॖ

This is replaced by *anusvAra* and ह gets a dot above:

हं

The next letter is *k* – क् which is followed by *A* to give *kA*, written:

का

Finally, the last letter, also encountered earlier, is the semi-vowel *r*, followed by *a* and written:

र

which completes the word –
अ + ह् + अ + म् (replaced by *anusvAra*) + क् + अ + र् + अ =
ahaMkAra – अहंकार

This then completes the first column of the 25 main consonants, the *sparsha vya~njana* – the guttural or *kaNThya* family.

2. The palatal or *tAlavya* consonants

The second group forms the sounds in the back part of the mouth but not the throat. Using the same tongue and mouth position as for the *i* vowel, these use the back of the tongue and the rear of the mouth; they are called 'palatal' or *tAlavya*. They follow the same pattern as the previous group (as do all five of these groups of consonants) in that the first and third members are *alpaprANa*, the second and fourth are *mahAprANa* and the fifth is *anunAsika*.

a) ch (or c), c

The first, with the letter *a* appended, is written:

च

The word *chit* refers to pure awareness or Consciousness, as in the word *sat-chit-Ananda*, more correctly written *sachchidAnanda* when the rules for combining words are taken into account, referring to the being-consciousness-bliss nature of the non-dual Absolute of Advaita. The word *chit* is written:

चित्

The *ch* is followed by *i* and the *virAma* after the letter *t* indicates that it is a pure consonant.

b) Ch (or chh), ch

The second character in the *tAlavya* group, *Cha*, is written:

छ

In 'everyday' speech, even by those who actually have some knowledge of Sanskrit, the difference in pronunciation between *ch* and *Ch* will probably be indistinguishable. *Ch* should have a little more breath following the un-aspirated 'ch' sound. *Chid* is spelt with a *Ch* and means 'to cut'.

छिद् – *Chid*

c) j, j

The third letter in this group (followed by *a*) is written:

ज

A simple example is the word meaning 'moving' or 'living' but more often used for 'world', 'humankind' or even 'universe' – *jagat*. This is written:

जगत्

Here you see *ja* and *ga* (both sounded with *a*) and a '*halanta*' *t* (i.e. with a *virAma* since this is not sounded with *a*).

d) jh, jh

The fourth letter, not a very frequently occurring one, is written (with *a* added):

झ

and the example used in Level 1 was *jhalA*, meaning 'girl':

झला

The letter form used by the Sanskrit–English dictionary looks rather different:

– as used in Monier-Williams' dictionary. [*Note that there are a few letter forms for which no computerized font could be found. This is one of them. Accordingly, they have been hand-drawn and scanned as image files and will not match the quality of the other characters.*]

e) ~n (or JN or J), ñ

The final letter in this group, with *a* appended, is the nasal:

ञ

This is another infrequent letter. It is also one which rarely exists, except in conjunction with another consonant. We can have the word meaning 'the letter ~*n*' as earlier:

अकार – ~nakAra

Although there is a separate section later on devoted to conjunct consonants, it will do no harm to introduce one here. The word *kA~nchana* means 'gold', 'money' or 'wealth' or, as an adjective, it means 'golden'. It is written:

काञ्चन – *kA~nchana* and the structure is easily seen:
का *(kA)* is followed by ञ् *(~n)* on top of च *(cha)* and then न *(na)*
The *~n* appearing above *cha* is pronounced *~ncha*. (If the *ch* were on top of the *~na*, then it would be pronounced *ch~na*).

3. The cerebral or *mUrdhanya* consonants

The third group forms the sounds with the tip of the tongue pointing up to the roof of the mouth. With mouth and tongue position similar to that for pronouncing the *RRi* vowel, they are called 'cerebral' or *mUrdhanya*.

All of this third (middle) group have a dot underneath the Romanized character including the ऱ vowel if you remember – this makes it easy to recognize the letter is *mUrdhanya*. None of the cerebral consonants are very common. Two pages of the 1300+ pages of Monier-Williams cover all of the words beginning with them. If ever in any doubt as to whether a 't', 'th', 'd' 'dh' or 'n' sound is cerebral or dental, put your bets on dental every time!

a) T, ṭ

This (together with *a* – definitely not going to repeat this for later consonants!) is written:

ट

This is more common in the middle of words and especially after the sibilant, *Sh*. Since the enjoyment of conjunct consonants is being reserved for later, however, here is a word without any:

टगर – *Tagara* – three simple letters, ट (*Ta*) ग (*ga*) and र (*ra*), joined together. Not a terribly useful word, though; it means 'squint-eyed'.

b) Th, ṭh

This character is:

ठ

The Katha Upanishad, one of the ten major Upanishads, has this letter, and its correct transliteration is *kaTha* and the *Th* is, in fact, a single letter and not two. *kaTha* literally refers to the name of a sage and founder of a school of philosophy. It is also worth mentioning here that, when we speak of this document, it should not strictly be 'Katha Upanishad' at all. It is normal for several successive words to be joined together in Sanskrit and if a Sanskrit word ending in a vowel is followed by one beginning with a vowel, there will usually be a change of some sort. Here, the 'a' and the 'u' combine to make an 'o' sound and the correct title is *kaThopaniShad*. The representation of this vowel will be dealt with in the next section, when we have completed the five main groups of consonants.

kaTha is written:

कठ

c) D, ḍ

This is written:

ड

If you are extremely alert, you will immediately notice that this character looks exactly like that for the nasal ~N in the first group (*kaNThya*) except that the dot to the right is missing. The word *Damaru* is a sacred drum, shaped like an hour glass, used by the god Shiva:

डमरु – *Damaru*

d) Dh, ḍh

This is written:

ढ

The word *DhAla* means a 'shield' – ढाल

e) N, ṇ

This is written:

ण

Note that it has its own 'built in' vertical to the right, which has nothing to do with its being sounded with an *a*.

ण्‍ – *N*; ण – *Na*; णा – *NA*; णि – *Ni* and so on.

The word *kaNa* is an adjective relating to anything very small, such as 'a grain of dust', 'a flake of snow', 'a drop of water' or 'a spark of fire':

कण – *kaNa*

This is another letter having an alternative form. Though less frequently encountered, it is the one used in Monier-Williams so you should learn to recognize it:

ण

4. The dental or *dantya* consonants

a) t, t
This is written:

त

and was seen earlier in *jagat* and *tagara*. The word *tad* means 'that' and, because a *d* frequently changes to a *t* at the end of a word (as will be discussed later), this word often appears as *tat*:

तत् – *tat*

b) th, th

The *mahAprANa tha* is written:

थ

The word *thUthU* means 'the imitative sound of spitting', while *thaithai* means 'the imitative sound of a musical instrument' (one wonders which!). We will meet the Devanagari representation for the complex vowel *ai* in a minute but here it is shown in combination with a consonant:

थूथू – *thUthU*; थैथै – *thaithai*

c) d, d

This is written:

द

not to be confused with the cerebral
ढ *Dh*

We have had the word Devanagari so many times now that it is about time you saw the actual Devanagari for it!

देवनागरी

Although we have not yet dealt with *v* and *r* in this section, we had *v* in *jIva* and *r* in *guru* and *kAra*.

d) dh, dh

This is written:

ध

and must not be confused with *gh*:

घ

If you inadvertently close the loop, joining it up to the bar at the top, thereby producing a *gh* when you really wanted a *dh*, then you can make a little 'knot' or circle at the junction with the horizontal line and this is then understood to be a *dh*. Some texts may use this variant, too, since it can avoid confusion if the ink becomes smudged, for example.

The word *dhana* means 'a prize' or 'any valued object':

धन – *dhana*

Thus, *dhanakAma*, for example, means 'desirous of wealth' or 'covetous' (*kAma* meaning 'desire', if you recall).

e) n, n

Finally, in this group, the *anunAsika* (sounded through the nose and throat) *na* is written, as you know:

न

and I think we have already had sufficient examples of this already. However, you might like to see what the word *anunAsika* looks like:

अनुनासिक

5. The labial or *oShThya* consonants

a) p, p

A very common letter. It is written:

प

The word *para* is translated as 'far, distant, remote' etc. and *parama* is the superlative, meaning 'most distant, remotest' etc. or 'best, most excellent' (or, somewhat incongruously, 'worst'). It appears in words such as *paramAtman*, meaning the supreme spirit.

पर – *para*;
परम – *parama*;

परमात्मन् – *paramAtman*
(the *tm* bit will be explained later).

b) ph, ph

This is written:

फ – a logical extension of *p* (for a change).
फल *phala*

Pedantically, this means 'fruit' (though it can also mean the seed of a fruit) but it more generally refers to 'outcome' or 'consequence' etc. This example was used in the first level, where it was given as *phalam*, with the additional example of *karmaphalam*, meaning specifically 'fruit of action'. Lest there should be confusion over endings here, it is worth mentioning a little about gender, although I do not intend to go into any detail.

There are three genders, as in languages like Latin and German – masculine, feminine and neuter – and, as in Latin, the endings change according to the part of speech. If you look up a word in the dictionary, the gender ending is not given. Thus, *phala* is spelt thus and indicated as 'n.' for 'neuter'. The 'nominative' case ending for this (i.e. the ending taken if the noun is the subject of a sentence) is, in fact, *am*. So, if you want 'fruit' to be the subject of a sentence (in the singular), the word to use is *phalam*.

c) b, b

This is written:

ब

An important word in Shankara's Advaita philosophy is *bAdha*.

This is the process whereby a previously accepted point of view or way of thinking is supplanted by a quite different one. The word used to translate it is usually 'sublation' or 'subration'. The classical example in the scriptures is that of seeing a piece of rope in the dark and believing it to be a snake. When a torch is brought to bear on the subject, the mistake is realized. Realizing the lake in a desert to be merely a mirage is an example of sublation:

बाध – *bAdha*

d) bh, bh

This is written:

भ

This is another of those letters without a complete bar across the top. The word *bhagavat* means 'fortunate, prosperous, happy' or 'glorious, divine' or 'holy' when applied to gods etc. (*bhagavad*, as in *bhagavad gItA* is the comparative form).

भगवत् – *bhagavat*

As with *dh* above, there is an option here to have the bar continuing across the top (thus joining up and making the letter look like a *m* below) and then drawing a loop or circle at the top. The presence of the circle would make it clear that this is *bh* and not *m*.

e) m, m

Finally, the *anunAsika* in this group is written:

म

64

We have seen this in several words, such as *maha*, *mAyA* and *Dam*.

6. Table of main consonants and corresponding vowels
   Here is the complete list of the five groups:

Table 4 – The Five Main Groups of Consonants (Devanagari)

kaNThya	*a*	*k*	*kh*	*g*	*gh*	*~N*
	अ	क	ख	ग	घ	ङ
tAlavya	*i*	*ch*	*Ch*	*j*	*jh*	*~n*
	इ	च	छ	ज	झ	ञ
MUrdhanya	*RRi*	*T*	*Th*	*D*	*Dh*	*N*
	ऋ	ट	ठ	ड	ढ	ण
dantya	*LLi*	*t*	*th*	*d*	*dh*	*n*
	ऌ	त	थ	द	ध	न
oShThya	*u*	*p*	*ph*	*b*	*bh*	*m*
	उ	प	फ	ब	भ	म

C. The Remaining Vowels

The Sanskrit term for the complex vowels (*e, o, ai, au*) is *saMyukta svara*-s. *saMyukta* means 'joined together' or 'combined'.

1. e, e

If you look back to the first level to remind yourself, you will recall that five more compound vowels are formed by combining the sounds of the three main ones, *a, i* and *u* . The first of these, *e*, is formed when *a* combines with *i*. It is written:

ए

and the word *eka*, meaning 'one', as a (declining) adjective, is:

एक

You can probably guess that, like the other vowels, this changes its appearance when following a consonant. With *i* and *I*, an extra vertical line was added to the left or right respectively and joined up to the preceding consonant. With *u* and *U* we had the figure 9 lying prone or supine respectively underneath the letter, and so on. In this case, the sign used to indicate *e* is a single left-tending mark above the letter, often called a 'flag'. *ke*, for example, is:

क् + ए = के

The *kena* Upanishad, then, is:

केन

2. ai, ai

The further combination of *e* with *a* gives rise to *ai*, written:

ऐ

which can easily be seen as being identical to the character for *e* with the addition of a single 'flag'. It can further be seen that this 'flag' is identical to the one used in conjunction with a consonant to indicate that it is sounded with *e*. It is logical therefore that, when we want to sound a consonant with *ai*, we simply use **two** flags. *kai* is then formed as follows:

क् + ऐ = कै

The word *shaiva* means 'relating to or belonging to the god

Shiva' or 'a worshipper or follower of Shiva'. We haven't met the Devanagari for *sh* yet but it should pose no obstacle as long as you note that the single vertical on the right of the letter is part of the letter and not an indication that it is sounded with *A*:

श् – *sh*; शा – *shA*; शैव – *shaiva*

3. o, o

This is the vowel resulting from the combination of *a* with *u* and is written:

ओ

(Note that, because this letter uses the same basic character form as for *a* – *A*, it appears differently in Monier-Williams, having the different version of *A* with a flag added.) The letter is rarely seen in this form since there are few words beginning with *o*. One obvious exception might be thought to be the word *om*, which most people, not just 'spiritual seekers', will have heard of. Occasionally, this will be seen in this form:

ओम्

Strictly speaking, this ought to be written:

ओ३म्

with the

३ (3)

sign indicating that the *o* should be sounded as 'prolonged' (*pluta*) and not simply as two measures but you are unlikely to meet it in this form. This word is so important that it actually has its own symbol, called the *praNava shabda* (*shabda* means 'word' or 'sound'):

You will probably recognize it (certainly Indians will since it is prominently displayed in India on all of the buses, among other things!). This symbol is generated in ITRANS by the characters *OM*.

praNu means 'to make a humming or droning sound'. If you have heard monks repeating it, you will understand why – the 'm' sound at the end is continued with a resonating humming sound. *OM* is the symbol for God and its purpose is to convey the sense of God's universality. Names are used to represent those objects, concepts etc. about which we wish to speak. All words are necessarily limited – after all, they invariably contain only a few letters of the alphabet. The name we give to God would ideally contain all letters and all ways of sounding them. *OM* achieves this by utilizing the scientific way in which the Sanskrit language is constructed. As has already been pointed out, all of the sounds originate with the basic sound of 'a', sounded by simply moving the vocal cords with the mouth wide open. All of the remaining letters use this with the mouth, tongue and lips being progressively modified. In fact, only the vowels actually sound; the purpose of the consonants is to curtail the sounding of the vowels in different ways.

Now, if the sound 'a' is made and continues to sound while the mouth is slowly closed, the sound made at the 'mid-point', as it were, is 'u'. If these two sounds are made together or, more practically speaking, if the sound corresponding to the mid-point between these two is made, the sound that emerges is 'o' (as in 'boat'). If the mouth continues to close while still making the basic sound, the ultimate sound when the lips come together is 'm'. Thus, bringing all of these aspects together, the sound that encompasses the entire range of possible sounds is '*a – u – m*'. When sounded in practice, this is '*OM*'.

It is not just a word, devised by someone in antiquity to represent a concept so that he or she could speak about it to another. It is THE word, as in 'In the beginning was the Word, and the Word was with God, and the Word was God' (Gospel of John 1:1). One of the major Upanishads – the *mANDUkya* – has the whole of its few 12 verses about this word. It says that the syllable *OM* **is** Brahman, reality itself. Each part of the word is identified with a different aspect of consciousness. *a* is the waking state, *u* the dreaming state and *m* the deep-sleep state. Together, *OM* represents that consciousness that forms the substratum of all three, effectively a fourth 'level' of consciousness called *turIya*. The word also represents the union of the three gods *vishNu* (a), *shiva* (u) and *brahmA* (m) in the Hindu religion.

Because the sound includes all possible sounds, it is present in or behind all other words – it can be regarded as the source of all other words; the seed from which they arise. This single word has the capacity to create all other words and thus represents the capacity of God to create all things in the world. It is a universal sound, not restricted to any religion. It is the 'AMEN' in Christianity. If you listen to the word being correctly sounded, the vibration continues after the sound of the word itself ends. This 'unspoken' sound is always there in the absence of other sounds (and of mental activity of any kind!) – *prANa*, the basic vitality of life itself. It is the sound at the end of meditation when the mind is perfectly still; the sound to which T. S. Eliot refers in his magnificent work 'The Four Quartets' (Ref. 13):

At the source of the longest river
The voice of the hidden waterfall
And the children in the apple-tree

Not known, because not looked for
But heard, half-heard, in the stillness
Between two waves of the sea.

But what happens when *o* appears in the middle of a word, as is much more common? Well, in common with what has been found throughout the language so far, we look for the distinguishing feature of the letter on its own. This looks like the letter *A* but has a single 'flag' added. We know how to make a consonant sound with the vowel *A* – we add a single vertical line to the right. Therefore, in order to make it sound with *o*, we add a single vertical line and a single flag.

क् + ओ = को – *k* + *o* = *ko*

We mentioned the word *yoga* in the first level as an example of the letter *y*. The Devanagari for this is:

योग

4. au, au

This results from the further combining of *o* with *a* and, in just the same way as *ai* was a sort of 'step further' than *e*, so *au* is formed by further modification of *o*. This modification is done in exactly the same manner – a second 'flag' is added to the character:

औ

(Again this uses the different form of *a* in the Monier-Williams dictionary.)

औदक – *audaka*

means 'aquatic' or 'watery'.

Following the example of *e – ai*, it should come as no surprise at all that, when *au* is joined to a consonant we drop the *virAma* sign and add a vertical bar and **two** 'flags' after the consonant to represent the *au*:

क् + औ = कौ – *k* + *au* = *kau*

The word *mauna* means 'silence':

मौन

5. M or .n, ṃ or ṁ

aM and *aH*, the *anusvAra* and the *visarga*, though two of the 16 *mAtRRikA*, are not really vowels but neither are they consonants. They are sometimes called *ayogavAha*, which means 'not belonging to', though paradoxically, since they actually need another 'real' letter in order to be able to sound them at all, they are also sometimes called *yogavAha*, 'belonging to'.

The *anusvAra* is written:

अं – *aM*

When it appears in conjunction with a consonant, this dot is how it is represented:

क् + अं = कं – *k* + *aM* = *kaM*

The *anusvAra* which is pronounced through the nose only is a replacement for *m* at the end of a word when the following word begins with a consonant other than the sibilants – *sh*, *Sh*, *s*, *h*. Sometimes it replaces the '*m*' within a compound.

The word *saMyoga*, for example, meaning 'conjunction' or 'combination', began as *sam-yoga*. The *m* is replaced by an internal *anusvAra* and is written as a dot above the *sa*:

संयोग

(We met *y* in *mAyA* and *s* in *anunAsika* but will deal with them more fully shortly.)

Remember from Level 1 that the *anusvAra* is optionally replaced by the *anunAsika* from the same family as the consonant that follows. Thus, if the consonant is *p*, *ph*, *b* or *bh* it will be replaced by *m*. If the consonant is *k*, *kh*, *g* or *gh*, it will be replaced by ~*N*; if *ch*, *Ch*, *j*, *jh*, it will be replaced by ~*n*; if *T*, *Th*, *D*, *Dh*, it will be replaced by *N*; if *t*, *th*, *d*, *dh*, it will be replaced by *n*. If the next word begins with a sibilant, then the *anusvAra* stays as it is, and when followed by *y*, *l*, *v* has the effect of nasalizing these consonants. The correct ITRANS representation is .*n* for all cases except the dental consonants.

The *anusvAra* is also a replacement for '*n*' when it is followed by *ch*, *Ch*, *t*, *th*, *T*, *Th*. Thus, it is not an independent nasal sound – it is an alternative sound for *m* or *n* in the circumstances described above.

6. H, ḥ

The *visarga* is written as a colon, usually after a vowel. Here it is shown after the letter *a*:

अः – *aH*
क् + अः = कः – *k* + *aH* = *kaH*

It was mentioned earlier that the ending of many masculine nouns, in the nominative case, is *aH*. Thus, the word *bAlaka*, for example, meaning 'child, boy or youth', is written *bAlakaH* if it is the subject of a sentence:

बालकः

visarga, like *anusvAra*, is not an independent sound. It is essentially the replacement for the final letter *s* of a word in certain circumstances – always, for example, if the word is the last in the sentence. Or you see it if the word is followed by *sh, Sh, s* as well as *k, kh, p, ph*.

7. *guNa* and *vRRiddhi*

When an *a* is 'added' to a simple vowel (*a, i, RRi, LLi* or *u*) the resulting vowel is said to be 'stronger' and is called *guNa*. [It is actually more complicated than this but the detail is beyond the scope of this book.] We saw above how *i* became *e* when added to *a*, and *u* became *o*. We also saw these being combined a second time with *a* to give *ai* and *au*, respectively. These second forms are even 'stronger' and are called *vRRiddhi*. The other simple vowels also have *guNa* and *vRRiddhi* forms, as shown in the following table. These become important when considering how part-words combine to form words. (This so-called 'internal *saMdhi*' is discussed shortly.)

Panini tells us that *guNa* is the name of the letters *a, e* and *o*; and *vRRiddhi* is the name for the letters *A, ai, au*.

Table 5 – *guNa* and *vRRiddhi* Form of Vowels

Basic *svara* form	*guNa* form	*vRRiddhi* form
अ, *a*	अ, *a*	आ, *A*
इ, *i*	ए, *e*	ऐ, ai
उ, *u*	ओ, *o*	औ, *au*
ऋ, *RRi*	अर्, *ar*	आर्, *Ar*
ऌ, *LLi*	अल्, *al*	आल्, *Al*

D. Table Showing the 16 *mAtRRikA*

Table 6 – The 16 *mAtRRikA* (Devanagari)

1	अ	आ	इ	ई	उ	ऊ	ऋ	ॠ
2	*a*	*A*	*i*	*I*	*u*	*U*	*RRi*	*RRI*
3	क	का	कि	की	कु	कू	कृ	कॄ

1	ऌ	ॡ	ए	ओ	ऐ	औ	अं	अः
2	*LLi*	*LLI*	*e*	*o*	*ai*	*au*	*aM*	*aH*
3	कॢ	कॣ	के	को	कै	कौ	कं	कः

The Devanagari letters appear in the first row in the form in which they would be written on their own or if appearing at the beginning of a word. In the second row is the ITRANS equivalent. In the third row is how they normally appear, when combined with a consonant, in this case *k*.

E. The Remaining Letters (semi-vowels, sibilants and *h*)

I will not repeat the discussion of the sounding of these letters and most of them have now been encountered earlier as part of other words. Instead I will simply give the Devanagari form of each letter and provide some more examples of their use. The Sanskrit for the semi-vowels incidentally is *antaHstha* and for the sibilants *UShman*, which also includes the letter *h* (which is called the 'aspirate'). *antaHstha* means 'being in the midst' or 'between', i.e. standing between the vowels and the consonants. *UShman* means 'heat', 'steam' or 'vapor', perhaps because these letters sound like escaping steam.

1. y, y

This is written:

य

We have seen this in words like
yoga योग
and *mAyA* माया

2. r, r

This is written:

र

and it behaves very well some of the time as in, for example, the word meaning 'delighted':

रत *rata*

There are a number of situations, however, in which it insists on forming special forms of its own. When sounded with *u* or *U*, it does not use the '9' shape underneath the letter as other consonants do. Instead, it takes new forms:

रॣ + उ = रु – *r* + *u* = *ru*

Note that the *virAma* appears underneath the *r* since it would cause confusion if attached directly to the ending of the *r*. The additional ornamentation to signify the *u* ending is similar to that used to change the vowel *u* to *U* – this may help you to memorize this special character.

$$\xi + \overline{\mathfrak{W}} = \overline{\mathfrak{K}} - r + U = rU$$

Here, the extra element added to *r* is the same as that used to signify *U* endings for other consonants (i.e. the prostrate '9') but moved up to the right of the letter instead of being underneath. An important concept in Advaita philosophy, applied to the visible, material universe, is that it is only 'name and form', *nama* and *rUpa*. *rUpa* is simply written:

रूप

(This noun is neuter, so you will also sometimes see it given as *rUpam*.)

r behaves the same as other consonants when followed by other vowels.

3. l, I

This is written:

ल

and we saw it in *laghu* and *DhAla* and *phalam*. The word *laya* means 'dissolution'; *pralaya* refers to the destruction of the world at the end of the Hindu *kalpa* (4320 million-year period):

लय – *laya*; प्रलय – *pralaya*; कल्प – *kalpa*

Note that, in *kalpa*, some of the right-hand section of the distinctive part of *la* disappears when it forms a conjunct with *p*. We will look at the topic of conjuncts very soon now. This is a foretaste!

4. v, v

This is written:

व

We saw it in *shaiva* and Devanagari. The name given to the character that appears under *halanta* consonants is *virAma* and is written:

विराम

5. sh, ś

The first of the sibilants, in the palatal position, is written:

श

and it is another of the letters that has a vertical line as part of the letter, not as an indication that it is sounded with *A*. It was seen in *shaiva* and is the *halanta* character in the verb 'to see, look at or observe':

पश् – *pash*

6. Sh (previously shh), ṣ

This cerebral sibilant is written:

ष

ShaSh is the number 6 – षष्

विषय – *viShaya*

This means 'sphere' or 'territory', 'period' or 'duration' but is used in the scriptures in the sense of the five 'objects of sense': *shabda*, sound, for the ears; *sparsha*, touch, for the skin; *rUpa*, form, for the eyes; *gandha*, odor, for the nose; *rasa*, taste, for the tongue.

7. s, s

The last sibilant, in the dental position, is written:

स

and is a very common letter. The word *sat* is the present participle of the verb *as*, 'to be', and is translated as 'being', 'existing', etc.

सत् – *sat*

8. h, h

The last letter of the alphabet, the 'aspirate', is written:

ह and it is seen clearly in
अहम् – *aham*, meaning 'I'.

F. The Complete Alphabet

Table 7 – The Complete Alphabet (Devanagari)

आ	ए	ऐ	ई	ऋ	ॡ	ऊ	ओ	औ		
A	*e*	*ai*	*I*	*RRI*	*LLI*	*U*	*o*	*au*		
अ			इ	ऋ	ऌ	उ			अं	अः
a			*i*	*RRi*	*LLi*	*u*			*M*	*H*
क			च	ट	त	प				
ka			*cha*	*Ta*	*ta*	*pa*				
ख			छ	ठ	थ	फ				
kha			*Cha*	*Tha*	*tha*	*pha*				
ग			ज	ड	द	ब				
ga			*ja*	*Da*	*da*	*ba*				
घ			झ	ढ	ध	भ				
gha			*jha*	*Dha*	*dha*	*bha*				
ङ			ञ	ण	न	म				
~Na			*~na*	*Na*	*na*	*ma*				
			य	र	ल	व				
			ya	*ra*	*la*	*va*				
ह			श	ष	स					
ha			*sha*	*Sha*	*sa*					

G. Conjunct Consonants

As we have seen above, consonants have no sound of their own and need to be joined to a vowel in order for a sound to become manifest.

The pure consonant *k* cannot be heard on its own, but here are the various vowels when sounded through the consonant *k*:

k (no sound), *ka, kA, ki, kI, ku, kU, kRRi, kRRI, kLLi, ke, kai, ko, kau*

क् क का कि की कु कू कृ कॄ कॢ के कै को कौ

The consonant can also become manifest in two ways without being followed by a vowel: it can be preceded by a vowel or it can be followed by another consonant. Examples of the first of these are: *ak*, *it*, *uk*, etc:

अक् इक् उक् etc.

This section provides some examples of the second type.

When two consonants combine without an intervening vowel, we need to write the combined letter in such a way as to know which of the consonants is 'pure' (*halanta*).

There are two main ways in which consonants join together. In the first of these the *halanta* consonant is 'cut' and positioned first (i.e. to the left); in the second way, it is placed on top.

When it is positioned on the left of the combination, it loses a bit of its right-hand side. Those consonants which have a vertical bar on the right-hand side simply lose this. Look at Table 7 to see how many this covers. In the first column, for example, we have *kha*, *g*, *gh*. When they lose their right-hand vertical, they look like this when combined with another consonant:

ख् ग् घ्

Guess what the following are:

ङ् च् ज् झ् ञ् ण् त् थ् द् ध् न् प् ब् भ् म् य् र् ल् व्

Those without right-hand verticals are just chopped off if possible. Examples of this truncation are *k*, *ph*:

क् फ्

Thus, you see, it is not nearly so bad as you might first think! Many do not change at all and, once you have realized which are the distinguishing features of each letter, you will easily see how just those parts are used in letter combinations. (Note that semi-vowels, sibilants and *h* are all regarded as consonants in this context.) If you have learned the basic letter forms, there is not much more to learn. You do not have to remember all of the possible conjuncts. If you are translating from Devanagari, you can see the conjuncts and work out what they are without too much difficulty. If you are writing Devanagari and using a tool such as Itranslator, it will generate the conjuncts for you.

Examples of the second type are where the *halanta* letter is placed at the top of the stack. See the following:

क्ल

You can recognize two consonants, *k* and *l* – one without the vowel *a* and the other followed by *a* – but you need to know how to pronounce it. Is it *kla* or *lka*? The answer is *kla* because the *halanta* consonant goes on top.

1. Vertical conjunct – *pa~nchadashI*

As an example of the second type of consonant conjunction, we will look at *pa~nchadashI*. This is a philosophical treatise on Advaita, based upon the Upanishads. The word itself literally means 'fifteen', because that is how many chapters it contains. The letter *~n* is immediately followed by a *ch* so the characters combine to form a conjunct consonant. The Devanagari for this word is therefore:

पञ्चदशी

This may look very complicated initially but is really quite straightforward. The first letter is

प – *p* + *a* sounded after it. Then comes the conjunct.

You can see the letter
~n, ञ् on top and
cha, च beneath.

The conjunct is followed by *a* and sounded *~ncha* – because the *halanta* consonant is the one on top, namely *~n*. Next comes the letter *d* followed by *a*:

द

Then comes *sh*, which you recall has a vertical line that does not mean it is sounded with *A*. This letter is joined by a 'hook' to another vertical line, meaning that it is sounded with *I* instead of *a*, i.e. *shI*.

At this juncture we can make another point about pronunciation. This is easier to do using the transliterated form of the word, *pa~nchadashI*. Break up the sound into its individual component letters as follows:

p a ~n ch a d a sh I

As we have said many times, the pure consonant needs to be appended to a vowel in order to be manifest. So far we have assumed that this can only take place if the vowel follows, but it can be achieved with a preceding vowel too. Looking at the letters above, we can join the *p* with the *a* to give *pa*. Then we have *~n* which is not followed by a vowel, so the only option is to join it to the preceding *a*. This now gives us *pa~n*. The next three consonants are each followed by a vowel to which they join; so the overall pronunciation is:

pa~n cha da shI

2. Vertical conjunct – *sha~Nkara*

The name of Shankara has been mentioned several times now. His name begins with the *sh* just mentioned. Though usually written as above in Anglicized form, the 'n' is not the dental variety. Since it is followed by *ka* (without an intervening vowel), it is going to be the *anunAsika* in the same group – the guttural *~N*:

शङ्कर – *sha~Nkara*

Note that the *~Nka* conjunct has a vertical format, with the *halanta ~N* on top of the *ka* and the natural form of both characters still visible. Also note that this word is quite often found in the form *shaMkara*, which is not strictly accurate. Though it is probably encountered more often in this latter form, it does not tell you how to pronounce it correctly. To stress the pronunciation rule, the nasal *~N* will need to join its nearest vowel, which happens to precede it, to become manifest as a sound. So we pronounce the word:

sha~N ka ra

3. Horizontal conjunct – *mithyA*

As an example of conjunction, where the *halanta* consonant appears to the left instead of above the consonant that is followed by a vowel, look at the word *mithyA*. This literally means 'incorrectly' or 'improperly' and is often used to refer to objects in the world. According to Advaita philosophy, we take these as being real and existing in their own right when, in fact, their assumed separate existence is the result of our imposing name and form upon what is really the undifferentiated Self. So they do exist at one level but are dependent for their existence on the existence of something else; i.e. they are not *absolutely* real. A metaphor often used is our thinking of a wave and water. Does the wave exist? Yes. Can it exist apart from water? No. Can water exist apart from the wave? Yes. Water is real; wave is *mithyA*.

mithyA is written मिथ्या in Devanagari.

mi will be recognized at the beginning of the word from the example of *milita* that was given when the letter *i* was introduced. The conjunct that follows is:

थ् + या = थ्या ; *th + yA = thyA*

i.e. the upright supporting the characteristic part of the letter *th* is dropped and the remainder of the letter is attached to the side of the next letter.

Although, from a visual perspective, the *th* is joined to the *yA*, from a pronunciation perspective it needs to be attached to the preceding '*i*':

mith + yA

4. The special case of *r*

It was seen earlier how *r* does not follow the rules when used with the letters *u* and *U*. That is not its only exceptional behavior. When it forms conjuncts in which it is the final letter of a group of consonants, it indicates its presence by the use of a short right-sloping diagonal under the left-hand side of the adjacent letter, e.g.

प – *pa*; प्र – *pra*; क – *ka*; क्र – *kra*; द – *da*; द्र – *dra*

For example, *prANa*, meaning literally 'breath of life' and encountered in the breathing exercises called *prANayAma*, is written:

प्राण

Note that, although in this combination the *p* looks 'full' and the *r* looks truncated, it is the *p* (being the letter 'on top') which is the *halanta* consonant and it is the *r* which is followed by the long vowel *A*. Lesson: don't be tricked by appearances!

When *r* forms a conjunct with *t*, both letters get adjusted from what one would expect. Take the example of the word *putra*, meaning 'son':

पुत्र

It is pronounced *put-ra*. The *t* is *halanta*. If we remember the above rules regarding the form that *halanta* consonants take when they join other consonants, we would expect the *t* to simply drop its right-hand vertical and appear:

t – त्

But it has had to be truncated even further in order to be on top of the letter *r* with which it is conjoined:

त् + र = त्र – *t* + *ra* = *tra*

This is a good point at which to mention that *halanta t* does sometimes truncate in this way when followed by *ta*, as in *sattva*, meaning 'truth':

सत्त्व

Note that, here, there are three consonants joining: *t*, *t*, *v* (see point 5 below). Accordingly, *sattva* will be pronounced:

sat tva

With some letters, this simple diagonal is deemed insufficient or liable to lead to ambiguity, so another slight variant is used that looks like a French circumflex with the point touching the bottom of the conjunct. Examples are:

ट्र – *Tra*; ठ्र – *Thra*; ड्र – *Dra*

When the *r* is the **first** letter of a conjunct consonant, there is another non-standard behavior. We met the word *kAma* when we looked at *k* in the first level of the book. It means 'desire' and should **not** be confused with the word *karma*, meaning 'action' (although *kAma* undoubtedly often does leads to *karma* in many cases!). The conjunct *mra* is written:

म्र

as in *dhUmra*:

धूम्र

meaning 'smoky', as you would have expected from what we have just discussed. The conjunct *rma*, however, is written:

र्म

and the word *karma* is:

कर्म

the *r* part is signified by the 'curl' shape, open to the right, above the consonant that follows it.

5. Conjuncts with more than two letters

The technical term for a conjunct consonant is *saMyoga*, which literally means 'joined together'. Although all of the ones encountered so far have been formed from just two consonants, there can be more than this. The same principles are used in constructing them. Thus, *achintya*, for example, meaning 'inconceivable', contains the conjunct *nty*, which is written:

न्　+ त्　+ य = न्त्य – *n* + *t* + *ya* = *ntya*:
अचिन्त्य – *achintya*

The significant part of *n* is attached to that of *t*, in turn attached to the *y*, which is the consonant followed by *a*.

To return to the discussion of the letter *r*, if it begins a conjunct of more than one other consonant, the 'curl' appears over the final one:

र्　+ ध्　+ व = ध्वं – *r* + *dh* + *va* = *rdhva*

If the *r* appears in the middle of a group of consonants, the short, diagonal stroke or 'circumflex' is used in the appropriate place:

ण्　ड्　र्　य = ण्ड्र्य – *N* + *D* + *r* + *ya* = *NDrya*

It is worth noting, incidentally, that a tool such as Itranslator will not always produce the conjunct form that you expect. There are some that are really quite complicated, such as that for *~Ngya*, for example:

It is understandable that there were insufficient codes available in a single, non-Unicode font to cope with all possible combinations. Accordingly, what was done was to break the conjunct up into parts. This one is reproduced as:

ङ्ग्य

instead of a single character. The conjunct *gya* is simply preceded by *halanta ~N*.

An example of a word with more than three consonants conjoined is *kArtsnya*, which has five. It means 'entirely':

र् + त् + स् + न् + य = त्स्न्य – *r* + *t* + *s* + *n* + *ya* = *rtsnya*
कात्स्न्य – *kArtsnya*

6. Special conjunct forms

A few letter combinations do not follow the general rules outlined above. Instead they form a unique character of their own.

a) *j* + *~n*

We had the word *j~nAna* in the first level. It is one of the words encountered very frequently by the spiritual seeker, and one of the most important ones, so we will look at it in more detail now. It means 'knowledge'. It is found in the 'yoga of knowledge' – *j~nAna yoga* – in, for example, the Bhagavad Gita. It is also found as *j~nAnI*, referring to one who practices *j~nAna yoga* or, more generally, to a 'person of wisdom' or 'sage', meaning one who has realized the Self.

ज् + ञ = ज्ञ (*j* + *~na* = *j~na*) – ज्ञान (*j~nAna*)

ITRANS also allows you to represent the *j~n* conjunct by either *GY* or *dny*. Thus *j~nAna* may be written *GYAna* or *dnyAna* if you prefer. This is probably because some people actually pronounce the word in that way. Because *~n* can also be represented by *JN* or *J*, there are two more ways of writing this word: *jJNAna* or *jJAna*. (Note that Itranslator Software 1.2.0.83 will not translate this last form correctly.)

b) *k* + *t*

bhakti yoga is the spiritual path whereby a god is worshipped and one who follows this path is called a *bhakta*. *bhakta* can mean 'served' or 'worshipped' but in this context means rather 'serving' or 'worshipping'. The *bha* part is straightforward but *k* and *t* form another special conjunct consonant. We have already seen *t* as the first half of a conjunct, where the left-hand part was simply tagged on to the following letter. Thus, if the conjunct here were *tka*, it would be written:

त् + क = त्क – *t* + *ka* = *tka*

However, this is the wrong order for *bhakta* and the conjunct must be different:

क् + त = क्त – *k* + *ta* = *kta*

This is not altogether intuitive and it is one of the conjuncts that just have to be remembered. The reason is simply that the right-hand curve of the *k* would interfere with the left-hand curve of the *t* if it were constructed in the usual horizontal combination and *t* does not lend itself to a vertical construction. Fortunately, although you might not be able to remember what the character is if you are trying to translate from Roman to Devanagari, when you see the word in Devanagari, you can usually work out what the character must be. Anyway, the complete word *bhakta* is written:

भक्त

and *bhakti* is: भक्ति

c) Conjuncts of *sh*

As with *g* and *N*, the Devanagari form of *sh* has a vertical line at the right so it would not be surprising to find that, when in conjunction with another consonant, it drops this vertical in the same way. Thus, in *shyAma*, meaning 'dark', this is what it does:

श्याम

Unfortunately, this is one of the few situations where this happens (*shsh* is another). More frequently, it assumes a single 'twist' shape as a 'characteristic part' and uses this in its conjuncts as shown below:

श्ल – *shla* as in श्लवन – *shlavana*,

which means 'lame' or 'limping'. NB: It would not be wrong, however, to write this:

श्लवन

श्व – *shva* as in श्वेताम्बर – *shvetAmbara*,

one of the schools of Jain philosophy. This shape is retained when combined with *ra*, too, where the diagonal line form of the latter is used:

श्र – *shra* as in श्रुति – *shruti*,

the 'revealed' truths of the Vedas, and with *na*:

श्न – *shna* as in श्नथित – *shnathita*,

meaning 'pierced' or 'transfixed'. Note that here the horizontal bar of the *na* has been pushed downwards. You may also see this with the bar still horizontal but lower down the stem. This script was, after all, handwritten and not generated by computerized typefaces when it was current and variations were inevitable. Again, the normal format, just dropping the vertical from *sh*, would not be wrong:

इनथित

d) Conjuncts of *Sh*

The key part of *Sh* is quite distinctive and it forms a number of conjuncts where the diagonal line simply fills in the 'unused loop' of the other character:

ष् + ट = ष्ट – *Sh* + *Ta* = *ShTa* as in *aShTan*,

which means 'eight':

अष्टन् – *aShTan*

But *Sh* is also another one of the characters that forms special conjuncts in some cases, which cannot be worked out using the usual rules – you simply have to learn them. One of these occurs after *k*:

क् + ष = क्ष – *k* + *Sha* = *kSha* as in क्षत्रिय – *kShatriya*,

the warrior class of the caste system in ancient Indian tradition. If this conjunct added another consonant, it would then drop the right-hand vertical:

e.g. क्ष् + व = क्ष्व – *kSh* + *va* = *kShva*

Another well-known example of the conjunct *kSh* is in
मोक्ष – *mokSha*,

meaning 'enlightenment' or, more accurately, 'liberation' in the sense of release from worldly existence. Because the conjunct sounds a bit like 'x', ITRANS allows you to use this instead and the word can be written *moxa*.

e) Conjuncts of *h*

Some of the conjuncts of *h* follow the usual pattern:

ह्म is *hma*, and ह्य is *hya* for example.

However, because of the unusual shape of the letter, it is clearly possible to put some 'key' letter elements *inside* the lower part of *h* to create some special 'vertical' conjuncts:

ह्ण – *hNa*; ह्न – *hna*; ह्व – *hva*; ह्र – *hra*.

You may also see *hra* with the diagonal to the left of the letter in the more usual way but this should pose no problem by now.

7. Table showing some common conjuncts
   Table 8 – Some Examples of Conjuncts
   Initial Letter Some Conjuncts

k	क्क	क्त	क्य	क्र	क्र्य	क्ष	क्ष्य
	kka	*kta*	*kya*	*kra*	*krya*	*ksha*	*kshya*
kh	ख्य	ख्र					
	khya	*khra*					
g	ग्य	ग्र					
	gya	*gra*					
gh	घ्न	घ्न्य	घ्म	घ्य	घ्र		
	ghna	*ghnya*	*ghma*	*ghya*	*ghra*		

~N	ङ्क	ङ्क्त	ङ्ख	ङ्ग
	~Nka	~Nkta	~Nkha	~Nga

ch	च्च	च्छ	च्म	च्य
	chcha	chCha	chma	chya

Ch	छ्य	छ्र
	Chya	Chra

j	ज्ज	ज्झ	ज्ञ	ज्य	ज्र	ज्व
	jja	jjha	j~na	jya	jra	jva

~n	ञ्च	ञ्छ	ञ्ज
	~ncha	~nCha	~nja

T	ट्ट	ट्य
	TTa	Tya

Th	ठ्य	ठ्र
	Thya	Thra

N	ण्ट	ण्ड्र	ण्ण
	NTa	NDra	NNa

t	त्क	त्क्र	त्त	त्न	त्म	त्र	त्स्न
	tka	tkra	tta	tna	tma	tra	tsna

d	द्द	द्ध	द्न	द्भ	द्म	द्य	द्र
	dda	ddha	dna	dbha	dma	dya	dra

dh	ध्न	ध्म	ध्र
	dhna	dhma	dhra

n	न्त	न्त्र	न्द्र	न्न	न्य	न्र	न्स
	nta	ntra	ndra	nna	nya	nra	nsa

p	प्त	प्त्य	प्न	प्र	प्व	प्स	प्स्व
	pta	ptya	pna	pra	pva	psa	psva

b	ब्द	ब्ध	ब्न	ब्र
	bda	bdha	bna	bra

bh	भ्न	भ्य	भ्र
	bhna	bhya	bhra

m	म्न	म्प्र	म्भ	म्र
	mna	mpra	mbha	mra

l	ल्क	ल्म	ल्ल	ल्ह
	lka	lma	lla	lha

v	त्न	व्य	त्र	व्व		
	vna	*vya*	*vra*	*vva*		
sh	श्च	श्न	श्य	श्र	श्ल	श्श
	shcha	*shna*	*shya*	*shra*	*shla*	*shsha*
Sh	ष्ट	ष्ट्र	ष्ण	ष्प्र	ष्य	
	ShTa	*ShTra*	*ShNa*	*Shpra*	*Shya*	
S	स्क	स्त्र	स्न	स्म	स्र	स्स
	ska	*stra*	*sna*	*sma*	*sra*	*ssa*
h	ह्ण	ह्न	ह्म	ह्य	ह्र	ह्ल	ह्व
	hNa	*hna*	*hma*	*hya*	*hra*	*hla*	*hva*

H. Some Special Characters

There are several special characters that you will also see when you look at Sanskrit texts. Two of these have already been dealt with, namely the *virAma* to signify a '*halanta*' consonant and the *praNava shabda* as the mystical symbol 'OM'. The single dot of the *anusvAra* above a consonant sounded with *M* and the double dot of the *visarga* after one sounded with *H* may also be regarded as special characters.

The *praNava shabda* itself is produced in ITRANS by either *OM* or *AUM*. The latter has the advantage of reminding us of the origin and symbolism discussed earlier when introducing the character *o*.

The sign over the OM symbol

which looks like a shallow concave bowl containing a dot, is called a *chandra-bindu*, meaning literally 'moon-like spot'. It is a sign that the vowel over which it appears should be nasalized, e.g.

which is written *a.N* in ITRANS and अं in Romanized transliteration. The concave shape on its own may also sometimes be
seen in old manuscripts where it functions the same as the
anusvAra. It is called an *ardhachandra*, meaning 'crescent-
shaped', and can be generated in ITRANS by writing '.c'. For
example:

संसार – *saMsAra*; सँसार – *sa.csAra* (Note that this second word
uses a different font – Mangal – because the one used for everything else (Sanskrit 98) will not reproduce the *ardhachandra*.)

The *chandra-bindu* is also used (in Panini's book of grammar,
the *aShTAdhyAyi*) in conjunction with the first letter of one of the
five groups of consonants to indicate that the whole group is
being referred to. Thus,

तुँ – *tu.N* – is an abbreviation used to refer to
त् थ् द् ध् न्
पुँ – *pu.N* – is an abbreviation used to refer to
प् फ् ब् भ् म्

A special case of the *chandra-bindu* occurs in conjunction with
a *virAma*, with no apparent associated letter at all. This is called
the 'Vedic *anusvAra*'. An example of this is found in the first
sutra of the Isa Upanishad (*IshopaniShad*):

ॐ ईशा वास्यमिदꣳ सर्वं यत्किञ्च जगत्यां जगत् ।
तेन त्येन भुञ्जीथा मा गृधः कस्यस्विद्धनम् ॥ १ ॥

I will not translate this in detail here. You will be able to work
out the beginning, however – *OM IshA* – and the next word
appears to be *vAsyamida* followed by a peculiar symbol. In fact,
the ITRANS code for this word is *vAsyamida{\m+}* and the
'{\m+}' code generates the *chandra-bindu* over a *virAma* instead
of an *anusvAra*. This signifies a special pronunciation – the

'Vedic pronunciation' – and, instead of pronouncing the word *vAsyamidaM*, if we simply used an *anusvAra*, it is pronounced *vAsyamidag~N*, i.e. the word is sounded with the *halanta*, guttural nasal sound instead of the generic, labial 'm'.

You should also note the single vertical line at the end of the first line of script and the two sets of double lines at the end of the second. The single line is called, somewhat confusingly, a *virAma*. It marks the end of a sentence or half-verse of a *sUtra*. The double line is called a *pUrNavirAma* and it marks the end of the *sUtra* or the end of a paragraph. These lines are generated by a full stop in ITRANS (i.e. one full stop produces one line). These are, in fact, the **only** punctuation marks in Sanskrit. There are no equivalents of semi-colons, question marks, exclamation marks or even quotation marks.

The complete ITRANS for generating the above *sUtra* is:

OM IshA vAsyamida{\m+} sarvaM yatkiJNcha jagatyAM jagat .
tena tyaktena bhu~njIthA mA gRRidhaH kasyasviddhanam.h ..
1 ..

You can see now that the other symbol that you probably did not recognize, between the two sets of double lines on the second line, is simply the numeral '1'. These are dealt with in Section I. (Note also that it is an accepted convention to use the '.h' variation of ITRANS to indicate a *halanta* consonant, when this occurs at the end of a sentence, even though the same Devanagari script is generated.)

The other special character, which you will see occasionally, is called an *avagraha* and is written:

ऽ

The *avagraha* indicates that an *a* letter has been dropped, in the same way as the apostrophe in English indicates that either 'o' or 'i' has been dropped, e.g. don't or it's. Observation will show that the letter preceding the dropped *a* is likely to be *o* or *e*. This is due to the requirement for euphonic flow, which will be dealt with later. The Roman transliteration in Sanskrit uses an apostrophe in just the same way as English to represent the *avagraha*. An example of an *avagraha* is found in the second line of the next *mantra* of the *isopaniShad*:

कुर्वन्नेवेह कर्माणि जिजीविषेच्छत‍ॱ समाः ।
एवं त्वयि नान्यथेतोऽस्ति न कर्म लिप्यते नरे ॥ २ ॥

On the second line, you should be able to read the words quite easily now. The first three are *evaM tvayi nAnyatheto*. Then there is an *avagraha* followed by *sti na karma lipyate nare*. Then there are two sets of double lines either side of the character for '2', identifying that this is the second *sUtra*. The reason for the *avagraha* is that the word actually following this symbol is *asti*, the third person singular of the verb 'to be' or 'to exist'. It means <the subject of the sentence> 'exists'. Because the preceding word is *nAnyatheto*, Sanskrit, always striving for the optimum efficiency in sound, does not want to sound *o* followed by *a*. There is no option available for combining the sounds, since *o* is itself already a combination. Accordingly, the *a* of *asti* is dropped and, to signify in the written version that this will occur when it is spoken, the *avagraha* is inserted. [Note that the word *nAnyatheto* began its life as *na anyathA itaH* but the words merge and the combined letters are forced to change as you will find out on the next Level when we discuss *saMdhi*.]

This second line, then, is written:

evaM tvayi nAnyatheto.asti na karma lipyate nare .. 2.. in ITRANS, with the '.a' generating the *avagraha*. In Romanized transliteration, it would be written:

evaṁ tvayi nānyatheto´sti na karma lipyate nare || 2 ||

A point to note here is that, just as one does not pronounce the missing 'o' in 'doesn't' so too one does not pronounce the missing 'a' in the above verse. That's why the apostrophe route is preferable in transliteration to prevent the temptation to reinsert the missing 'a' sound.

I. The Numerals

Roman numerals actually derive from the Sanskrit originally so that some similarity of the figures can easily be recognized. The principal situation in which they will be needed is in Devanagari references to *sUtra*-s in some scriptural texts. They are shown in the following table:

Table 9 – The Devanagari Numerals

१	२	३	४	५
1	2	3	4	5
eka	*dvi*	*tri*	*chatur*	*pa~nchan*

६	७	८	९	
6	7	8	9	
ShaSh	*saptan*	*aShTan*	*navan*	

Level 3 Some Practical Examples

A. *shivasUtrANi*

(These are also sometimes called the '*maheshvarANi sUtrANi*'.)

* * *

Do not be apprehensive about the Sanskrit text that appears below! There are no words or pronunciation to be worked out. Each verse only contains a short string of the letters that you have just learned in Level 2 but in a particular, meaningful sequence. And all will be explained! Furthermore, you do not need to know anything about the *shivasUtrANi* in order to learn the Sanskrit language. If you prefer, you may learn the rules for sandhi as a list of do's and don'ts. I am introducing these partly because they are a useful reinforcement for letter recognition and partly for interest.

* * *

Another very helpful way to gain familiarity with the alphabet is to learn by rote a set of short verses (*sUtra*-s) that contain all of the letters. These are very special verses in that the ordering of the letters within them enables groups of letters quickly and easily to be identified in a shorthand way. Then it is possible to apply a set of rules that determine such things as how letters at the end of a word will combine with those at the beginning of the next.

This is best understood by seeing (and learning!) the *sUtra*-s and seeing how they operate. Otherwise, the abstract concept may be difficult to grasp. The sheer ingenuity and cleverness with which they and their associated rules were constructed is quite staggering. The system was developed by the Sanskrit grammarian Panini in his book *aShTAdyAyI*, about 2,500 years ago. There are about 4,000 sutras covering the entire grammar. The specific verses relating to the letter groupings are called the *maheshvarANi* sutras because Panini is supposed to have had a dream in which *maheshvara*, referring to the 'great Lord or God' was playing the sutras on a drum. There are 14 sutras or *sUtrANi* – *sUtrANi* is the plural of *sUtra*. They are all very short, since they are made up not of words but of the letters of the alphabet. Two of them contain only two letters. Consequently, they are relatively easy to learn. (The word *maheshvara* is itself a good example of the application of one of the rules to be described below regarding the changing of vowels at the end/beginning of words when they are adjacent. It derives from the two separate words *maha*, meaning 'great' and *Ishvara*, meaning 'Lord'. When *maha* joins with *Ishvara*, the *a + I* becomes *e*.)

Each *sUtra* consists of one or more 'active' letters of the alphabet and terminates in an 'inactive' letter, referred to as an '*it*' *varna* (*varna* means 'letter' or 'sound'). The key feature of these *it* letters is that they are not seen (although still exerting some influence). For this reason, they are also called 'indicatory' letters – they indicate something, but are distinct from what they indicate.

1) अइउण् – *a-i-u-N* – i.e. the main vowels (*a, A, i, I, u, U*) (active) terminating in the (inactive) *halanta* cerebral nasal *N*
2) ऋऌक् – *RRi-LLi-k* – i.e. the (active) vowels at the cerebral and dental positions terminating in the (inactive) *halanta* consonant, *k*
3) एओङ् – *e-o-~N* – i.e. the two (active) compound vowels, made by combining *a* with *i* and *u* respectively, terminating in the (inactive) *halanta* consonant *~N*
4) ऐऔच् – *ai-au-ch* – i.e. the remaining compound vowels (active), made by combining *a* with *e* and *o* respectively,

terminating in the (inactive) *halanta* consonant *ch*

5) हयवरट् – *ha-ya-va-ra-T* – i.e. three of the four semi-vowels, together with the 'aspirate' *h* (all active), terminating in the (inactive) *halanta T*

6) लण् – *la-~N* – i.e. the remaining semi-vowel (active), terminating in (inactive) *halanta ~N*

7) ञमङणनम् - *~na-ma-~Na-Na-na-m* – i.e. the five *anunAsika* consonants (active), terminating in (inactive) *halanta M*

8) झभञ् – *jha-bha-~n* – i.e. the second *mahAprANa* consonants in the palatal and labial groups (active), terminating in (inactive) *halanta ~n*

9) घढधष् – *gha-Dha-dha-Sh* – i.e. the second *mahAprANa* consonants in the other three groups (guttural, cerebral and dental) (active), terminating in (inactive) *halanta Sh*

10) जबगडदश् – *ja-ba-ga-Da-da-sh* – i.e. the second *alpaprANa* consonants in each of the five groups of consonants (active), terminating in (inactive) *halanta sh*

11) खफछठथचटतव् – *kha-pha-Cha-Tha-tha-cha-Ta-ta-v* – i.e. the first *mahAprANa* consonants in each of the five groups and three of the first *alpaprANa* ones (active), terminating in the (inactive) *halanta v*

12) कपय् – *ka-pa-y* – i.e. the remaining two first *alpaprANa* consonants (active), terminating in the (inactive) *halanta y*

13) शषसर् – *sha-Sha-sa-r* – i.e. the three sibilants (active), terminating in the (inactive) *halanta r*

14) हल् – *ha-l* – i.e. the aspirate (active), terminating in (inactive) *halanta l*

Learning this will take some effort but can be used to great advantage for those wishing to study Panini's grammar, because he used this version of the alphabet to create a shorthand way of expressing his grammatical rules. If written, it will help tremendously in learning the alphabet. If spoken, it will quickly be realized that this requires considerable agility of the tongue and is excellent for learning correct pronunciation. Naturally this does necessitate that you have at least a recording of how it **should** sound and preferably someone who can listen to you and correct mistakes.

Below is the complete set of शिवसूत्राणि (*shivasUtrANi*) or महेश्वराणि सूत्राणि (*maheshvarANi sUtrANi*):

अइउण् ऋलक् एओङ् ऐऔच् हयवरट् लण् अमङणनम् झभञ् घढधष् जबगडदश् खफछठथचटतव् कपय् शषसर् हल्

and now we'll have a brief look at the purpose of combining the letters in this way, and the role of the indicatory '*it*' letters.

Specific groups of letters can be identified by a two-letter code. Thus, for example:

a) अण् – *aN* is shorthand for the first three primary vowels. It is derived from the first *maheshvarANi sUtra*, '*a-i-u-N*'. The first letter of this sUtra is *a* and the last is *N*. Thus the whole batch can be indicated by the shorthand, which starts with the first and ends with the last letter of the batch: *aN*. As we have said, the letter *N* is called '*it*' and this means that it is not seen. What this unseen letter means is that the batch being indicated are the letters *a*, *i*, *u*. That is how it comes to be a shorthand for 'the three principal vowels'. NOTE: there are seven syllables in saying 'the-three-prin-ci-pal-vow-els' and only one in saying 'aN'. We have therefore saved six syllables by using this shorthand. In Panini's day, the grammarian's art was to express their rules in the most succinct way and so the saving of even a single syllable was valued; it is said, as highly as the birth of a son! Saving six must be a great achievement.

b) अक् – *ak* similarly is shorthand for 'the five simple vowels'. The batch starts with '*a*' and ends with the unseen indicatory letter '*k*' with the unseen indicatory letter '*N*' in between. So, discounting the unseen letters, *ak* is the shorthand for *a, i, u,*

RRi, LLi.

c) अच्– *ach* – identifies all vowels. The letter *a* begins the first *sUtra* and *it halanta 'ch'* occurs at the end of the fourth *sUtra*. Discounting all of the 'inactive' or '*it*' letters (i.e. those at the end of each *sUtra*), the (active) letters are: *a, A, i, I, u, U* (first *sUtra*); *RRi, RRI, LLi, LLI* (second); *e, o* (third); *ai, au* (fourth).

d) अल्– *al* – identifies all of the letters from *a* at the beginning of the 1st *sUtra* to *h* in the last (excluding all inactive letters). The shorthand '*al*', therefore, stands for the whole alphabet.

e) हल्– *hal* – identifies all of the consonants, from *h* at the beginning of the fifth *sUtra* to *h* (again) at the beginning of the final *sUtra* (again, as always, excluding inactive letters). Now you can see the reason for the word *halanta*. This refers to the situation in which a consonant (i.e. *hal*) occurs at the end (i.e. *anta*) of a word.

f) यण्– *yaN* – refers to the semi-vowels, from *y* as the second letter in the fifth *sUtra* to *l* as the only active letter in the sixth.

g) एच्– *ech* identifies the compound vowels, from *e* as the first vowel in the third *sUtra* to *au* as the last active letter in the fourth.

h) शर् – *shar* – identifies the three sibilants, from the thirteenth *sUtra*.

i) शल् – *shal* – identifies the four *UShman* letters (three sibilants + *h*).

j) And so on! Each of these two-letter abbreviations is called a *pratyAhAra* in Panini's book on grammar and there are 42 of them altogether. In fact, another name for these sutras is *pratyAhAra sUtrANi*.

(If you are inordinately alert, you may have realized that *aN* could refer either to <*a, i, u*> or to <*a, i, u, RRi, LLi, e, o, ai, au, h, y, v, r, l*>. In fact, Panini explains, in a note to one of his sutras, that it should always be interpreted as the former, except in the sutra to which the note refers.

Also, if alert, you will notice that one 'active' letter occurs twice: the letter '*h*'. This might explain its double status – sometimes grouped with the semi-vowels and sometimes with the sibilants.)

B. Words and Sandhi

1. Words

All Sanskrit words derive from short 'root' words, each of which is called a *dhAtu*, and there are only about 2,000 of these. When looking up a word in the dictionary, its origins will often be identified as a *dhAtu* and this will be specified by a 'square-root' sign √ appearing in front of it. The *dhAtu* itself appears in the Monier-Williams dictionary in slightly larger, bolder font than other words and is in Devanagari form (whereas derived words are shown in Roman transliterated form). The *dhAtu*-s are quite fundamental and many of our own English words can be traced back to them. An example is *sthA*, meaning 'to stand', 'take up a position', 'remain', 'persevere' etc. If you know Latin, you will probably recognize *sto, stare, steti, statum* – the verb 'to stand'. English words such as 'stay', 'station' and so on derive from this.

In order to form meaningful words from the *dhAtu*, 'affixes' are added – i.e. prefixes and suffixes – usually only of one or two syllables. These endings (prefix or suffix) are called *pratyaya*-s. How these syllables are added, and what effect this has on existing vowels, is very precisely codified in the grammar.

The *dhAtu-s* are grouped into ten families, and the way in which the evolution of each *dhAtu* takes place will be according to the rules applying to the family in which they occur. For example, in some families the vowel is replaced by its *guNa* or *vRRiddhi* form before the addition of affixes. In other cases there is a duplication of a particular letter, and so on. These changes to the *dhAtu* produce the stem form of the word, the *prAtipadika*, the form that will be found in the dictionary. It has also been mentioned, however, that these stem forms need to go through one more set of changes before they become a word, *pada*, which is a meaningful unit in a sentence.

Words are formed by adding further endings to the *prAtipadika*. These endings are of two types: one set of endings gives us verbs and their derivatives, and the other set gives us nouns. Here is where the proliferation begins!

Let us start with nouns: These are divided according to gender (feminine, masculine and neuter), according to number (singular, dual, plural), and according to case, i.e. the role in the sentence.

There are seven case endings accounting for the noun's role in the sentence. The noun could be the subject of the action (doer), object of the action, instrument by which the action is accomplished, that to which the action is directed, that from which it proceeds, that in which the action is located, or it could be that which possesses another noun in the sentence (as in the student's headache, where the headache created by all this proliferation is possessed by the student).

This is not where the proliferation ends. The fixed set of 21 case endings will depend not only on the gender of the noun, but also on the letter with which the *prAtipadika* ends. In respect of basic noun endings, if the *prAtipadika* ends in *a*, the noun is likely to be masculine, in which case the standard ending will be modified in a particular way. The nominative (subject) endings of these nouns, for example, are likely to be *aH*. If, however, the *prAtipadika* ending in *a* happens to be neuter gender, then the nominative form will end in *am*. Thus, *phala* is *phalam* (neuter) while *nara* (meaning 'man' and clearly masculine) is *naraH*. The *prAtipadika*-s (in the dictionary) ending in *A* or *I* are almost always feminine, e.g. *mAyA*, *nAdI* (a river). The nominative singular of *mAyA* is *mAyA* and of *nadI* is *nadI* so there is no confusion here at least. Then we can also have *prAtipadika*-s ending in *i* or *u* or *RRi*, which could be any gender. And, of course *prAtipadika*-s can end in a variety of consonants: *Atman* is an example of the *prAtipadika* ending in *n*, where the nominative singular is *AtmA*.

If we next turn to verbs, we have an equivalent list of factors that influence the verb endings. First, there are number (singular, dual, plural), and person (first, second, third). These two in combination give us a table with 3 x 3 = 9 forms. This then doubles to 18, because verbs can be in two main classes: directed towards the other, *parasmaipada*, or directed towards oneself, *Atmanepada*. These 18 forms will then vary according to time (present, past and future – plus subtle variations of these latter two) and mood (e.g. command, request, option, etc).

This is how, with a handful of seeds and a handful of laws, Sanskrit manages to grow a vocabulary that is massively rich in meaning and lawful in its development.

Incidentally, the 21 case endings of nouns are called *sup-vibhakti* or *namavibhakti* (name-endings) and the 18 verb endings are called *ti~N-vibhakti* or *kriyAvibhakti* (action-endings).

As an example, the *dhAtu* '*nI*' means 'lead, guide, direct' etc. The preposition (called an *upasarga* in Sanskrit) '*apa*' means 'away, back, off'. Thus the verb *apanI* means to 'lead away, lead off' or 'rob, steal' etc. If this occurs in a sentence such as 'he leads away' for example, it then adds the appropriate *kriyAvibhakti* ending and becomes '*apanayati*'. Thus *rAjAnamapanayati* – 'he leads away the king'. *rAja* is the *prAtipadika* form found in the dictionary, meaning 'king'. Since it is in the accusative (the king is the object of the leading away), it adds the second, singular *namavibhakti* ending and becomes *rAjAnam*.

This book assumes that you really do not want to go into this level of detail. The section on 'Resources on the Internet' will provide information on how to pursue this study further.

2. Pronunciation

Having learned how to pronounce each letter, the pronunciation of words follows naturally. Letter sounds do not change when they are part of a word as they often do in English. The sounds are always distinct and discrete even when in combination with other letters. Thus, for example, there are no situations such as an 's' sound and a 'h' sound becoming a 'sh' sound when they occur together. They will retain their own unique sound and simply follow one another.

Stressing certain syllables within words when they are spoken is as critical in Sanskrit as it is in English. The rule is straightforward and depends upon whether a syllable is 'light' (*laghu*) or 'heavy' (*guru*). Long vowels (*dIrgha*) or any vowels immediately preceding a cluster of consonants, a *visarga* or an *anusvAra* are heavy, and the stress is placed on these. Short vowels that are not one of the special cases just mentioned are light and no stress is placed on them. Thus: *anúsvÁra, visárga, sáMyúkta, prátyÁhÁra, prÁtipadika, mahéshvara, avágraha, upániShat*. To understand the difference, take any of these words and pronounce them according to your inclination; then pronounce them by laying the stress on the syllables with the acute accent. One way to get the textural variation is to sound the unstressed syllables softly and the stressed ones loudly one at a time and then, once you have the stresses in the right places start to close the gap, e.g.

A nús vÁ ra, vi sár ga, sáM yúk ta, prát yÁ hÁ ra.

Other commonly mispronounced words are:

ar ju na, ma hÁ bhÁ ra ta, pra kRRi ti (no stresses at all)

When a mantra text is chanted, a secondary factor is added, namely accent. There are three main accents: high, *udÁtta*; low, *anudAtta*; raised, *svarita*. Below is an example of an annotated text. The underlined letters are sounded low (*anudAtta*); the unmarked should be sounded higher in relation to them (*udAtta*); and those with a single vertical line above them are the highest of the three notes (*svarita*). In some places there is a double vertical above a letter (*dIrgha svarita*): this is sounded with a high followed by a low note. The safest way to understand all of this is to work with a traditional teacher.

ॐ भद्रं कर्णेभिः शृणुयाम देवाः । भद्रं पश्येमाक्षभिर्यजत्राः ।

स्थिरैरङ्गैस्तुष्टुवाꣳ सस्तनूभिः । व्यशेम देवहितं यदायुः ।

स्वस्ति न इन्द्रो वृद्धश्रवाः । स्वस्ति नः पूषा विश्ववेदाः ।

स्वस्ति नस्ताद्र्क्ष्यो अरिष्टनेमिः । स्वस्ति नो बृहस्पतिर्दधातु ॥

om   bhadram   karṇebhiḥ   śṛṇuyāma   devāḥ | bhadram
paśyemākṣabhiryajatrāḥ | sthirairaṅgaistuṣṭuvāṁ sastanūbhiḥ |
vyaśema devahitaṁ yadāyuḥ | svasti na indro vṛddhaśravāḥ |
svasti naḥ pūṣā viśvavedāḥ | svasti nastārkṣyo ariṣṭanemiḥ |
svasti no bṛhaspatirdadhātu | |

ॐ शान्तिः शान्तिः शान्तिः ॥

om śāntiḥ śāntiḥ śāntiḥ | |

3. Joining words and part-words

When speaking or writing Sanskrit, words are joined wherever possible within a sentence or line of poetry. Pauses in speech or breaks in written words within a sentence normally only occur when a word ends in a vowel, a *visarga* or an *anusvAra* and the next word begins with a consonant. Go back to the invocation mantra above and note where the breaks are. A good example is the famous saying (*mahAvAkya*) from the Chandogya Upanishad '*tat tvam asi*', meaning 'that thou art'. The first word ends in a consonant, the second begins with a consonant; so no break. The second ends in a consonant, the third begins with a vowel; so no break: it is therefore written:

तत्त्वमसि – i.e. as one continuous expression, *tattvamasi.*

Note that the word for 'that' is actually *tad* but for the sake of euphonic flow, *saMdhi*, it is changed to *tat* because it is followed by *t*.

Sandhi (actually *saMdhi*) refers to the way in which letters (i.e. sounds) change when they are joined together in a continuous flow of speech. It is also sometimes called 'euphony' because the purpose of the whole exercise is to end up with a harmonious-sounding sentence. Panini also uses the word *saMhitA* for this, defined as 'the closest drawing together of sounds'.

If the letters in question are at the end of one word and the beginning of the next, the joining is referred to as 'external sandhi'. If they refer to the joining of parts of a word, it is called 'internal sandhi'. Unless you are studying the language seriously, it is the external variety that is most important, since written words can be difficult to decipher without an understanding of how the component words may have changed. There can also be sandhi of vowels or of consonants. The former is called *ach saMdhi* (*ach* being the *pratyAhAra* for all the vowels, as explained above); the latter is called *hal saMdhi*, since *hal* identifies all consonants. A third set of rules come into play when a *visarga* is followed or preceded by various letters.

It is worth remembering that the sole purpose of sandhi is to make the language sound as harmonious as possible. This is not a phenomenon restricted to the Sanskrit language. In English, for example, it is so much easier to say 'an apple' than 'a apple'.

Internally, too, English has sandhi. The letter 's' is pronounced 'sss'. When appended to the word 'cat' – cat*s* – it retains its 'sss' sound. But when appended to 'dog' – dog*s* – the s is pronounced 'z': dogz. When appended to horse – horse*s* – not only is the 's' pronounced 'z' but the 'e' of horse is sounded as though it is 'i': hors*iz*. In English we make these changes in pronunciation only and not in writing. In Sanskrit, we change both the spelling and the pronunciation. If the English grammarians were formulating spelling rules, they might have one that says: when 's' follows 'd', it is replaced by 'z', but retains its true nature when following 't'.

Where the conjunction of two letters makes the words difficult to pronounce or if the result sounds awkward, there will be a rule for combining the letters to get around the problem. Knowing this can sometimes enable you to make a good guess at what is needed, if you are forming the word, or at what has happened, if you are trying to read it. Not all of the Sanskrit rules of euphonic harmony are being given here – there are quite a lot of them, including exceptions and special cases. But, unless you are seriously studying the language, it is not necessary to learn them anyway. Once the principles have been understood, much of it becomes common sense. Very often, you can hear what the result should be simply by speaking the two separate words quickly in succession.

Sandhi can be analyzed into three categories: vowel, *visarga* and consonant. In each category, a number of rules can be specified to enable one to determine what will happen when a word or part-word ending in a specific letter joins with another word or part-word beginning with a specific letter. Many of the rules have sub-rules to cover special cases and exceptions. After a particular rule has been applied and the end character of the first word, say, has been changed accordingly, it may then happen that another rule comes into play for this new character and a further change must take place. Thus, several stages may be involved in the progressive modification of endings until a result is reached which sounds 'harmonious'. For you to learn all of these rules and become familiar with their operation is not the intention of this book. The following paragraphs merely offer a flavor of the topic and a later section will refer you to other resources that you can follow up if you wish to.

The WebPages on Rules of Sandhi, from the Argentinian site (see 'Resources on the Internet', Section B) list 7 primary and 7 secondary rules for the joining of vowels, 10 rules involving *visarga* endings and 24 rules for joining consonants, some of which have anything up to 6 sub-rules. (Incidentally, I cannot recommend these WebPages too highly. Although Panini is not mentioned, all of the rules are presented in a very methodical and detailed manner with many examples. It is very readable and easy to understand.)

4. Some examples of vowel sandhi

a) Coalescence of similar vowels

This is the simplest form of sandhi, showing what happens when a word ending in one of the five main vowels (short or long) joins a word beginning with the same vowel. There is a sutra in Panini's book of grammar to describe this: *akaH savarNe dIrghaH* (Literal translation: 'In place of *ak* when followed by *savarNa* there is a long measure.')

It says that whenever an *ak* sound (i.e. *a, A, i, I, u, U, RRi, LLi*) is followed by a *savarNa* sound (meaning 'of the same family' i.e. a **similar** sound), the two vowels are replaced by the *dIrgha* form, i.e. the long form of the vowel. Thus, if a word ending in *a* or *A* is followed by one beginning with *a* or *A* (the 'similar' sounds), they are joined and both of the joining vowels are replaced by a single occurrence of *A*. If a word ending in *i* or *I* joins one beginning with *i* or *I*, both joining vowels are replaced by one *I*. And so on. Thus *kapi* means 'monkey' and *indra* means 'prince' (among other things). These join to become *kapIndra* (lord of monkeys), with the two *hrasva i*-s becoming a *dIrgha I*. Similarly, *kuru* refers to an ancient country or region, probably north of the Himalayas, and *uttama* means 'best, highest, greatest, chief, etc.'. These two combine to produce *kurUttama* with the two *hrasva u*-s becoming a *dIrgha U*.

b) Coalescence of dissimilar vowels when the first is *a* or *A*

Providing that the last vowel of the first word is *a* or *A*, coalescence with a beginning vowel of the second word occurs in a similar manner to the table of *guNa* and *vRRiddhi* discussed earlier, except that, as in a) above, the length of the two vowels does not matter. Thus *a* or *A* joining with *i* or *I* produces *e* as in *mahA* (great) + *Isha* (lord) = *mahesha* (great lord). *a* or *A* joining with *RRi* or *RRI* produces *ar* as in *mahA* (great) + *RRiShi* (sage) = *maharShi* (great sage). *a* or *A* joining with *e* will produce *ai*, and with *o* will produce *au*. If *a* or *A* joins with *ai* or *au*, it will produce *ai* and *au*, respectively, since these are the 'full extent' of coalescence, as it were.

c) Coalescence of dissimilar vowels when the first is **not** *a* or *A*

This is covered by the first of the sutras relating to the joining of vowels in Panini's book of grammar: *iko yaNachi*. (Literal translation: 'In place of *ik* letters there are *yaN* letters.') Its meaning is as follows:

If a word ending in *i, u, RRi* or *LLi* is immediately followed by a word beginning with any vowel other than itself (in the same sentence or in the same line of a poem), then the *i, u, RRi, LLi* is replaced by *y, v, r, l* respectively and the two words will then be written and sounded as if they were one. Thus, *vi* and *a~njana* combine to form *vya~njana*. The *i* is replaced by the semi-vowel in the same group (palatal). If you sound the two words together, the *i-a* naturally turns into a *y* so it is all perfectly logical.

d) Coalescence when first vowel is complex

The first Panini sutra relating to this situation is *echo.ayavAyAvaH*.

This is similar to *iko yaNachi* but now refers to a word ending in *ech*, i.e. *e*, *o*, *ai* or *au*, joining a word beginning with *ach*, i.e. any vowel. The ending vowel of the first word is replaced by *ay*, *av*, *Ay* or *Av*, respectively. This is essentially what happens if this situation occurs within a word, i.e. at the joining of two parts of a word. It is a little more complex if there are two separate words. As has already been seen, for example, if a word ending in *e* or *o* is followed by one beginning with *a*, the *a* is dropped but the words remain separate and an *avagraha* is inserted. Also, y's and v's produced as a result of this coalescence can optionally be dropped.

Something very noticeable about the sutras in Panini's grammar is their extreme conciseness. This frequently seems to occur to an extreme of complete unintelligibility. The brevity is intentional, the incomprehensibility presumably not! The situation is not actually as bad as it appears at first sight. What happens is that many of the sutras occur in groups, each of which is called an *adhikAra*, meaning 'topic' or 'subject'. The elements of the topic are introduced logically, one bit at a time but, once a point has been made, it is not repeated. Entire words introduced in a sutra earlier in the topic are assumed still to apply and we have to mentally 'bring them down' from the earlier ones as necessary. The principle is called *anuvRRitti*, which means the 'continued course or influence of a preceding rule on what follows'. The same principle applies to Vyasa's sutras in the Brahmasutras, for example.

5. Some examples of consonant sandhi

As mentioned above, there are many more of these. We will look at just six main ones. These are applied in the order given so that, if after applying one, a subsequent rule also becomes applicable, then it is applied too. (We never go back to the beginning on reaching the end, you will be glad to hear!)

The purpose of all of these rules of sandhi is to maximize the harmony and avoid any inharmonious conjunction of sounds. Vowels and consonants, in addition to the various categories already given earlier, are said to be either 'soft' or 'hard'. Another word for 'soft' is 'unvoiced', as compared to the 'hard' ones, which are 'voiced'. This categorization refers to the fact that the vowels (except for the *visarga*) and consonants in the first two rows (*k, ch, T, t, p, kh, Ch, Th, th, ph*) do not make the sound of a syllable. There is no soft resonance; they make a hard, clipped sound and are therefore 'unvoiced' or *aghoSha*. The remainder of the consonants (last three rows), together with *H*, all sound like short syllables, soft or 'murmuring', and are said to be 'voiced' or *ghoSha*. It is an aim of these *saMdhi* rules that conjunctions of hard and soft should be avoided. For example, if a word ending in a hard sound is followed by a word beginning with a soft one, the hard letter has to be changed to a soft one so that the resultant joining sound is harmonious.

a) Word ending in any consonant other than a nasal or a semi-vowel

The *pratyAhAra* for 'any consonant other than a nasal or a semi-vowel' is *jhal*, if you look back at the discussion of the *maheshvarANi sUtrANi*. The rule relating to this is that, when a word ending in a *jhal* consonant joins another word, the *jhal* consonant is replaced by the corresponding *jash* consonant. *jash* is the *pratyAhAra* for *j, g, b, D or d* i.e. a consonant from the third line of the five groups of consonants, the second set of *alpaprANa* consonants. The sutra is:

झलां जशोऽन्ते – *jhalAM jasho.ante*

An example would be:

sat (real, true) + *guru* (teacher) = *sadguru*

Here, the first word ends in the dental *t*, which is a *jhal* consonant. Since it is followed by another word, we have to replace it with the corresponding *jash* consonant, i.e. the one in the same group as the *t*, namely the dental *d*.

b) Joining of a dental consonant with a palatal

The Panini sutra relating to this situation is *stoH shchunA shchuH* and, expanded into something vaguely meaningful, it says the following:

A स्तुँ (*stu.N*),
when this joins with a श्चुँ (*schu.N*),
is replaced by another श्चुँ (*schu.N*)

The meaning of these terms was explained when we discussed the *chandra-bindu* in Level 2 Section H:

तुँ – *tu.N* – is an abbreviation used to refer to
त थ द ध न

Therefore, *stu.N* in Panini's system of abbreviations means 'either an *halanta s* or any of the *tu.N* letters', i.e. any *halanta* dental consonant *t, th, d, dh, n*. Similarly, *shchu.N* means *halanta sh* or any of the *halanta* palatal consonants (*ch, Ch, j, jh* or *~n*). So, if a word ending in *halanta s, t, th, d, dh, n* is followed by a word beginning with *sh, ch, Ch, j, jh, ~n*, the dental consonant is replaced by the corresponding palatal.

e.g. *tapas* (religious austerities) + *shivaH* (favorable, auspicious) = *tapashshivaH*

The dental *s*, being followed by the palatal *sh*, is replaced by the corresponding palatal, i.e. *sh*.

c) Joining of a dental consonant with a cerebral

The corresponding rule when a dental (including *s*) meets a cerebral consonant (including *Sh*) is analogous. The Panini sutra is even more terse, using *anuvRRitti* as discussed earlier: *ShTunA ShTuH*. Following the same principle as before: when a word ending in *halanta s, t, th, d, dh, n* is followed by one beginning with *Sh, T, Th, D, Dh, N*, the dental consonant is replaced by the corresponding cerebral one. (Note that the dental consonant is not mentioned at all in the sutra – this part is the one that is 'brought down' from the earlier one. Note that it is the 'meeting' of the consonants that is being described. The same principle is followed if the first word ends in a cerebral and the next word begins with a dental.)

For example, *rAmas + TIkate* (Rama moves) becomes *rAmaShTIkate* with the dental *s* being replaced by the cerebral *Sh*.

d) When the second word begins with a nasal

The sutra here is *yaro.anunAsike.anunAsiko vA*. Remember that the '.' in the middle of a word in ITRANS refers to an *avagraha*, which means that the 'a' following the '.' is not sounded. This sutra states that, if a *yar* letter occurs at the end of a word, when the following word begins with a nasal consonant (*anunAsika*), then it can be (optionally) replaced by another nasal. *yar* is the *pratyAhAra* for all consonants except *h*.

Thus, *etad* (this) + *maya* ('made of, consisting of', not to be confused with *mAyA*) = *etanmaya* ('consisting of this'). The *d* at the end of the first word is a *yar* consonant so is replaced by the nasal in its same group (i.e. dentals: *t, th, d, dh, n*), *n*.

e) When a *jhal* letter is followed by a *khar*

This sutra is *khari cha* and is understood as 'Replace a *jhal* letter with a *char* if it is followed by a *khar*.' The *jhal* is 'brought down' from the earlier sutra. *khar* refers to consonants excluding nasals, semi-vowels and *h*. *char* covers *ch*, *T*, *t*, *k*, *p*, *sh*, *Sh* and *s*.

एतद् + संधि = एतत्संधि

etad (this) + *saMdhi* ('joining' business that we are investigating) = *etatsaMdhi*

The *d* of *etad* is a *jhal* consonant and is followed by *s*, which is a *khar*. Accordingly, it is changed to *t* (being the first letter in the group to which it belongs).

There was an example of this in Level 2 Section B 2a), when we saw that the three words *sat* and *chit* and *Ananda* became *sachchidAnanda*. The combination of the first two words is an example of the successive operation of rules. Here, the *t* at the end of *sat* is a *jhal* letter (consonant other than a nasal or a semi-vowel). Accordingly, it has to be replaced by the corresponding *jash* consonant. The *sat* + *chit* then becomes *sad* + *chit*. Now the second of the above rules comes into play. The *d* is a *stu.N* consonant while *ch* is a *schu.N*. So the *d* has to be replaced by the corresponding letter from the palatal group, which is *j*. Thus, *sad* + *chit* has now become *saj* + *chit*. Finally, this situation corresponds to that covered by the sixth rule. *j* is a *jhal* letter and *ch* is a *khar*. Therefore, the *j* must be replaced by a *ch*, the first letter of the (palatal) group. Thus the complete sequence is:

सत् + चित् becomes सद्चित्
becomes सज्चित् becomes सच्चित्

6. Samasa (*samAsa*)

This was mentioned briefly at the beginning of Level 2, to give one of the explanations for the very long 'words' that are often found in Sanskrit. The word actually means 'throwing or putting together' but also 'succinctness, conciseness'. In the context of grammar, it is understood to mean a 'compound word' but it probably has elements of both the literal aspects. It is very common, to the extent that possibly most sentences will contain at least one *samAsa*.

It may sometimes seem that many words, adjectives and nouns, are 'thrown together' to make an artificial new word but the fact that this can be done freely makes the language extremely versatile and able to express the most subtle ideas of an imaginative mind. The resultant word can summarize exactly what the author wishes to say in a concise and apt manner. And the resultant compound is treated as a word in its own right, with only the part at the end of the compound (which is always the principal word) needing to decline and change its endings.

Because all endings other than that of the principal noun (or adjective) are dropped, it is the word order within the compound that determines the relationship of one word to another, rather than the 'part of speech'. Normally just the 'stem' forms of words other than the principal one are used. (Of course, the part-words join together following the principles of sandhi.) An example given by Goldman and Sutherland (Ref. 4) is as follows:

जनकतनयास्त्रानपुण्योदकन् *janakatanayAsnAnapuNyodakan*

This word will not be found in Monier-Williams! It is actually made up of five words as follows:

जनक – *janaka*,
the famous king in Hindu mythology;
तनया – *tanayA*,
daughter (*tanayaH* is son);
स्त्रान – *snAna*,
bathing, washing, anything used in ablutions;
पुण्य – *puNya*,
auspicious, pure, holy;
उद्कन् – *udakan*,
water.

'Water' is the last word in the compound so this is the 'principal' word. The order of 'importance' or applicability of the other words then passes back one at a time. Thus the type of water that is being spoken of is 'holy' water; the type of holy water that is referred to is 'that used for bathing'. The provenance of this holy bathing water is 'that belonging to the daughter' and, finally, it is 'Janaka' about whose daughter we are speaking.

If this compound occurs in a sentence as an object, as for example, 'He drank the holy bathing water of Janaka's daughter', then only the last bit of the word would change its ending to the accusative (*-udakam*). All of the rest of the word would remain unchanged.

C. The Four *mahAvAkya*-s

mahAvAkya means 'great saying' – *maha* = 'great', *vAkya* = statement or assertion, and *maha* adds the extra *a* since *vAkya* is a feminine noun and the endings have to agree. There are four 'great sayings' from the Vedas that are said to encapsulate the teaching of Advaita Vedanta. This is the non-dualistic philosophy that claims that there are 'not two things', that there is only Brahman, the Absolute or Consciousness, and we are that.

a) The first of these, from the *aitareya* Upanishad in the *RRig* Veda, is:

प्रज्ञानंब्रह्म – *praj~nAnaMbrahma* –
Consciousness is Brahman

praj~nAna is a neuter noun, hence the *m* ending (which changes to an *anusvAra* because the next word begins with a consonant). *brahma* is 'Brahman' obviously. The two words are joined since the first does not end on a syllable. The verb is omitted from the 'sentence' and, this being the case, the word 'is' (*asti*) is understood.

b) The second, from the *ChAndogya* Upanishad in the *sama* Veda, has already been mentioned in B 3:

तत्त्वमसि – *tattvamasi* –
Thou art That

The three *pada*-s *tad* (that), *tvam* (you), *asi* (second person singular present indicative of the verb 'to be', i.e. 'you are') are joined into a single spoken and written word. The use of the pronoun *tvam* is for emphasis – **You** are That (i.e. Consciousness)

c) The third quotation is from the *mANDUkya* Upanishad in the *atharva* or *AtharvaNa* Veda:

अयमात्मा ब्रह्म – *ayamAtmA brahma* –
This Self is Brahman
ayam (this one), *AtmA* (the nominative singular ending of the masculine noun *Atman* meaning the 'individual self'). Again the verb (*asti* – 'is') is omitted – this is very common in Sanskrit.

d) The fourth of the sayings is from the *bRRihadAraNyaka* Upanishad in the *yajur* Veda:

अहंब्रह्मास्मि – *ahaMbrahmAsmi* –
I am Brahman

aham (personal pronoun 'I'), *asmi* is the first person singular present indicative of the verb 'to be' – 'I am'. The use of *aham* is for emphasis – **I** am Brahman. Again, the *m* of *aham* changes to *M* because the next word begins with a consonant.

D. Some Vedic Prayers and Quotations
For practicing reading Sanskrit, any of the Upanishads or scriptures such as the Bhagavad Gita are suitable. Many versions

of these contain the original Sanskrit, together with a transliteration and a literal translation. Some even contain a breakdown of the Sanskrit with the meanings of individual words.

(To my knowledge, there are several versions of the Bhagavad Gita which provide word-by-word breakdown – Refs. 14, 15 and 16 but only 14 has the Devanagari; the others only provide transliteration. Refs. 14 and 16 only give translations, whereas Ref. 15 also has an extensive commentary.)

It may be that you would prefer to study and learn a few key passages of especial beauty and/or philosophical meaning. If this is the case, there are quite a number of these and, of course, different people will point you to their own favorites. Below are a few of my own favorites.

1. 'Lead me from the unreal' from the *bRRihadAraNyaka upaniShad*

असतो मा सद्गमय । – *asato mA sadgamaya |*
तमसो मा ज्योतिर्गमय । – *tamaso mA jyotirgamaya |*
मृत्योर्मा ऽमृतं गमय ॥ – *mRRityormA.amRRita.n gamaya ||*

Lead me from the unreal to the real,
Lead me from darkness into light,
Lead me from death to immortality.

sat has been met before. It is an adjective and means 'real, being, existing, true etc.' The prefix *a* always negates the noun so that *asat* means 'unreal etc.' 'From' the unreal means that the adjective has to take the fifth case ending (called 'ablative', for those who studied Latin), which would make it *asataH*. The personal pronoun *aham* – 'I' – changes to *mAm* or *ma* in the accusative – 'me', the object of the verb 'to lead', *gam*.

Because *asataH* is followed by an *m*, which is a 'soft' consonant (see under B. 5 above), the *visarga* is changed to *u*, which immediately combines with the preceding *a* to become *o*.

Accordingly, *asataH mA* becomes *asato mA*.

The verb is in the imperative – 'Lead!' and I want to be led 'to the real', which is usually indicated by using the second case ending (i.e. indirect object having the same ending as the direct object for verbs expressing motion). 'To the real' is therefore *sat* but, this being followed by *gamaya*, the *t* changes to *d* in accordance with the rule *jhalAM jasho.ante* as described above. Thus *asato mA sadgamaya*.

tamas means 'darkness, ignorance, illusion etc.' I want to be led out of this, so the noun takes the ablative case ending, *tamasaH*. This changes in exactly the same way as did *asataH* above. This time I want to be led 'into light'. The Sanskrit for 'light' is *jyotis*. The accusative case is *jyotiH* but a rule of (*visarga*) *saMdhi* states that 'when a *visarga* is preceded by any vowel (except *a* or *A*) and followed by a vowel or a soft consonant, it has to be changed into an *r*'. Accordingly, with the *jyotiH* being followed by *gamaya*, the combination becomes *jyotirgamaya*. Thus *tamaso mA jyotirgamaya*.

The (masculine) noun for 'death' is *mRRityu*. Again this has to go into the fifth case ending, which is *mRRityoH*. Thus, following the same rule as before, when this combines with *mA* ('me'), it becomes *mRRityormA*. *amRRita* means 'immortality'. This is a neuter noun and the accusative case ending is *-am* so the *pada* is *amRRitam*. It has been mentioned earlier that an *m* is usually changed into an *M* when it occurs at the end of a word. The relevant Panini sutra is *mo.anusvAraH*. There is some *anuvRRitti* involved as well, obviously, and the complete instructions are that, in place of *halanta m* at the end of a fully inflected word when the next word begins with a consonant, *anusvAra* is substituted. Since the following letter is the *g* of *gamaya*, the *m* of *amRRitam* is therefore changed to *M*. Thus *mRRityormA amRRitaM gamaya*. In addition, it is pronounced the same as the *anunAsika* of the same group as the letter beginning the following word, i.e. ~*N*. Because *mRRityormA* ends in *A* and is followed by a word beginning with *a*, the *a* is elided and an *avagraha* is inserted to show that this has happened.

2. 'That is perfect' from the *IshA upaniShat*

This is the very famous introductory 'invocation'. The Upanishad occurs in the initial section of the Yajur Veda, which is unusual in that Upanishads normally occur at the end (hence *vedAnta – veda anta –* 'end of the Vedas'). The first sutra begins *IshA vAsyamida{\m+}*, if you recall (the text was given in Level 2 H, when we looked at the *chandra-bindu*), and the document is also sometimes called the Isavasya Upanishad.

ॐ पूर्णमदः पूर्णमिदं पूर्णात् पूर्णमुदच्यते ।
पूर्णस्य पूर्णमादाय पूर्णमेवावशिष्यते ॥

This, then, is the 'invocation'. It is often referred to as the 'Perfect Prayer', for reasons that will become apparent.

There will be no difficulty with the first word, *OM*. This was described in Level 2, C3 and H. The second word is *pUrNamadaH*. *pUrNa* means 'complete, entire, fulfilled etc' and is often translated as 'infinite' or 'perfect', though neither of these words is actually given in Monier-Williams. *adas* means 'that' as opposed to *idam* (which occurs in the next word), which means 'this'. As usual, the verb 'to be' is omitted throughout and understood to be present wherever necessary, so that this second word is translated as 'this is complete' (or 'perfect' or 'infinite'). The first rule of *visarga saMdhi* is that words ending in *s* can be changed to an *H*.

The next word, then, is *pUrNamidaM* and, as just explained, this means 'that is complete'. The *m*, being at the end of a word, is changed to *M*, as was explained in *asatoma* above. (The *m* ending on the adjective *pUrNa* is the neuter ending in the absence of any qualifying noun.)

The next word is *pUrNAt*. This is another example of the fifth (*pa~nchami*) or ablative case, this time for the adjective *pUrNa*, in the singular, masculine, meaning 'from the complete'. Now perhaps we can see why writers choose to use a word like 'perfect' or 'infinite' – 'from perfect' will sound much better.

The last word on line 1 is *pUrNamudachyate*. The verb *ach* means 'to go or move'. The prefix *ud* means 'up' or 'upwards' in the sense of superiority, so that *udach* would mean something like 'to promote'. The ending, however, is the passive voice, so it is translated as 'is manifested' or 'comes out of'. The clause therefore means that *pUrNam* or 'perfect' is manifested from perfect.

The next line begins with *pUrNasya*, the genitive case, meaning 'of the complete or perfect'. This is followed by *pUrNamAdAya*. *AdAya* at the end of a word has the sense of 'taking or seizing' so the two words together literally mean 'taking the perfect of perfect'. Next comes *pUrNameva* – just or exactly (*eva*) that same completeness or perfection (*pUrNam*). *avashiShyate* comes from the verb *avashiSh*, meaning 'to remain' and means 'it remains', being in what is called the 'middle voice' (*Atmanepada* or 'word for one's self'). This clause therefore means that, when the 'perfect of perfect' is taken, perfect remains.

Altogether, then, the prayer can be translated:

This is perfect. That is perfect. Perfection is manifested from the Perfect. When this perfection is taken from the Perfect, the Perfect still remains.

3. 'I do nothing at all' from the *bhagavadgItA*

नैव किञ्चित्करोमीति युक्तो मन्येत तत्त्ववित् ।
पश्यञ्शृण्वन्स्पृशञ्जिघ्रन्नश्नन्गच्छन्स्वपञ्श्वसन् ॥ ५।८ ॥
प्रलपन्विसृजन्गृह्ह्णन्नुन्मिषन्निमिषन्नपि ।
इन्द्रियाणीन्द्रियार्थेषु वर्तन्त इति धारयन् ॥ ५।९ ॥

These are the eighth and ninth verses from chapter 5 of the Bhagavad Gita. The length of the 'words' in the second and third lines might seem to be enough to put anyone off the study of Sanskrit. In fact, they are quite straightforward, as will be seen, and the overall profundity of these verses makes them worth the effort.

The first word of line 1 is *naiva*. This is simply a combination of the words *na*, meaning 'not' and *eva*, 'truly' or 'even'. Then comes *ki~nchitkaromIti*. *kim* + *chid* becomes *kiMchid*, meaning 'somewhat' or 'a little'. The alternative representation is because the *M* is spoken as though it were the *anunAsika* of the same group as *ch*, i.e. *~n*. *karomi* is the first person singular present indicative of the verb *kRRi*, 'to do'. *iti* means 'thus', if anything, and is very frequently used in Sanskrit simply to stress what has just been said or instead of quotation marks, since these do not exist. Putting these together, *karomi* + *iti* = *karomIti* and *kiMchid* + *karomIti* = *kiMchitkaromIti*. The *d* changes to a *t* in accordance with the sutra *khari cha* as discussed in B 5e) above. The first two words therefore translate as 'I do not even a little'.

The next word is *yukto*, from the adjective *yukta*. This comes from the same root as *yoga* and can mean 'yoked' or 'joined'. Here, however, it means 'absorbed in abstract meditation' and refers to a sage. It is the subject of the whole sentence, in the nominative masculine singular, *yuktaH*. The *visarga* changes to -*u*, because it is preceded by an *a* and followed by a soft consonant, and then *au* changes to *o*, producing *yukto*. Then comes *manyeta* from the verb *man*, 'to think', and is the 'optative' tense, meaning 'he should think'. The next word is *tattvavit*. We have already seen *tad* + *tvam* (that + you) in *tattvamasi*. Here, *tattva-vid* means 'knowing the true nature of'. The 'hard' or 'voiced' *d* of *tad* has to be replaced by the corresponding 'soft' or 'unvoiced' one, i.e. *t* since the next word *tvam* begins with a soft consonant. *tattvavid* becomes *tattvavit* for the same reason (this is the end of the sentence) and the rest of the first line is therefore *yukto manyeta tattvavit* – 'the sage, knowing the true nature of (the Self), should think'.

The second line, though appearing as a single word, is obviously not. The transliteration is:

pashya~nshRRiNvanspRRisha~njighrannashnangachChansv apa~nshvasan

In fact, it is just a succession of present, active participles of verbs describing what the speaker is (outwardly) doing when, in fact, the Self is not doing anything at all. Each one is rendered in the masculine, nominative singular:

pashyan – seeing (*n* changes to ~*n* on joining according to *stoH shchunA shchuH*)
shRRiNvan – hearing
spRRishan – touching (*n* becomes ~*n* on joining according to *stoH shchunA shchuH*)
jighran – smelling
ashnan – eating
gachChan – going
svapan – sleeping (*n* changes to ~*n* on joining according to *stoH shcunA shcuH*)
shvasan – breathing

The double 'n' at the end of *jighrann* results from the following rule of *saMdhi*: When ~*N*, *N* or *n* are at the end of a word and preceded by a short vowel, they must be doubled if followed by a vowel.

The third line continues this list of 'activities':

pralapanvisRRijangRRihNannunmiShannimiShannapi
pralapanan – talking
visRRijan – sending or letting go

gRRihNan – seizing (with the mind)
unmiShan – the act of opening the eyes
nimiShan – closing the eyes
api – (emphasis) even or also

The double 'n' at the end of *gRRihNann* and *nimiShann* results
from the *saMdhi* rule given above. That at the end of *unmiShann*
results from the rule: 'If a consonant (other than *h*) comes after a
vowel and is not followed by a vowel, it is optionally doubled.'

The last line is:

indriyANIndriyArtheShu vartanta iti dhArayan

The first part-word is *indriyANi*, the (nominative) plural of
indriya, referring to the five sense organs. The remainder of the
word is from *indriyArtha*, meaning a sense object. The ending is
the seventh case, plural (more than two, *bahu-vachana*) and
indicates where the action of the verb takes place, being translated as 'in', 'at' or 'among' etc. The next word, *vartanta*, is the
saMdhi change from *vartante*. Because *vartante* is followed by a
word beginning with a vowel other than *a*, the *e* changes to *ay*
and then the *y* is (optionally) dropped. *vartante* is the third
person plural present indicative from the verb *vRRit* meaning 'to
surround or enclose', usually referring to armies. Here, the
subject of the verb is *indriya*, the five sense organs – they are
'surrounding' the sense objects. The role of *iti*, meaning 'thus'
etc., has already been mentioned earlier. *dhArya* means
'maintaining, holding or possessing (the belief that)'. Therefore,
the Sage (who thinks 'I do nothing at all') maintains the belief
that the senses surround the sense objects.

Therefore, the complete translation is:

Believing that it is merely the senses surrounding the objects
of sense, though seeing, hearing, touching, smelling, eating,
going, sleeping, breathing, talking, mentally grabbing or letting

go, even just opening or closing the eyes, the Sage, knowing the true nature of (the Self) should think, 'I do nothing at all.'

4. 'You are not the body' from the *aShTAvakra gItA*

न त्वं देहो न ते देहो भोक्ता कर्ता न वा -वान् ।
चिद्रूपोऽसि सदा साक्षी निरपेक्षः सुखं चर ॥

This is chapter 15, verse 3 of the Astavakra Gita, an uncompromising treatise on Advaita Vedanta. Most of the words end on a syllable, so there is much less *saMdhi* apparent than in the earlier examples.

न त्वं देहो – *na tvaM deho*

na: not, nor, neither etc., used especially in repetition, as in this sentence, 'neither this, nor this etc.'

tvaM: *tvam* is the nominative singular of the personal pronoun 'you', already met several times. The letter *m* at the end of a word is always changed into an *anusvAra* when it is followed by a consonant.

deha is 'the person or individual', the 'outward appearance or form'. In the nominative singular, it is *dehaH* but, as was noted above, when the *visarga* is preceded by *a* and followed by a soft consonant, it changes to *u* and then the *a* and *u* combine to form *o*. This, then, simply means: 'you (are) not the body'. The verb *asi* is, of course, omitted as usual.

न ते देहो – *na te deho*

te is the sixth (genitive) case of *tvam* and means 'of or belonging to you – i.e. yours'. *na* and *deho* translate as before. This, then, means 'nor (is) the body yours', *asi* again being understood.

भोक्ता कर्ता न वा -वान् – *bhoktA kartA na vA bhavAn*

na vA is translated as 'neither … nor' though, unlike in English, *vA* doesn't usually come before the word to which it refers. *bhoktA* is the nominative masculine singular of the word *bhoktRRi*, which means 'one who enjoys or experiences'. Similarly *kartA* is from *kartRRi*, 'one who makes or does'. *bhavAn* is another word meaning 'you', again nominative singular, from *bhavat*. It is a much more formal version, though, often being translated as 'your honor' or 'your worship'. Perhaps there is an intentional irony here. You, who think yourself an important 'doer' or 'enjoyer', are in fact not even a body. I'll translate it with artistic license as 'Sir, you are neither an enjoyer nor a doer'.

चिद्रूपोऽसि – *chidrUpo.asi*

chit means 'pure thought, spirit, soul' but in the context of Advaita is usually translated as Consciousness, in the sense of Brahman. *rUpa* means 'form, outward appearance etc.' The *t* at the end of *chit* becomes a *d* in accordance with *jhalAM jasho.ante*. *chidrUpa* means 'the Universal Spirit as identified with pure thought' and the nominative singular is *chidrUpaH*. *asi* means 'you are'. When the two words combine, the *visarga*, being preceded and followed by an *a*, changes to *u* and, since this is (still!) preceded by *a*, the *a* and *u* combine to form *o*. The *a* of *asi* is now elided when speaking, but to show that it is still effectively present, an *avagraha* is inserted when it is written. The phrase is translated as 'you are Consciousness itself'.

सदा साक्षी निरपेक्षः – *sadA sAkShI nirapekShaH*

This is a continuing description of what you are. *sAkShI* is the masculine nominative singular of *sAkShin*, meaning a 'witness' and this is qualified by *sadA*, meaning 'always, perpetually' and *nirapekShaH*, meaning 'desireless, indifferent'. *asi* is understood again. Overall translation: 'you are the eternal, disinterested witness'.

सुखं चर – *sukhaM chara*

sukha means 'comfortable, happy, prosperous'; the nominative singular ending *m* is converted to *M* as before. The verb *char* can mean 'to move or travel through, to follow, behave, act, live etc.' and *chara* is the imperative. Exercising a little artistic license again, I would translate this simply as 'be happy!'

The complete translation, then, is:

You are not the body, nor is the body yours. Sir, you are neither an enjoyer nor a doer; you are Consciousness itself – the eternal, disinterested witness. Be happy!

5. 'All beings exist in me' from the *bhagavadgItA*

No apologies for this second extract from the Gita – this is another famous passage. It is one constantly being quoted by a friend and I am taking this opportunity to examine it in more depth!

सर्वभूतस्थमात्मानं सर्वभूतानि चात्मनि ।
ईक्षते योगयुक्तात्मा सर्वत्र समदर्शनः ॥

This is chapter 6, verse 29.

The verb of the sentence is ईक्षते – *IkShate* – third person, singular, present indicative of the verb *IkSh*, 'to see'.

सर्वभूतस्थमात्मानं – *sarvabhUtasthamAtmAnaM*

There are only two words conjoined here, *sarvabhUtastham* and *AtmAnaM*. *sarva* means 'all, every, manifold' etc. *bhUta* is 'that which is or exists, any living being (divine, human, animal or vegetable)'. *stha* means 'standing, staying, abiding, being situated in etc.'. There are not, however, three separate words here. (If there were, you would be wondering why the endings of words did not agree with apparent adjectives or why nouns appeared to be in the wrong case.) The single word *sarvabhUtastha* simply means 'present in all elements or beings'. *Atman* has been met already. *AtmAnam* is the singular, accusative, the object of this clause; the *-m* ending changes to *-M*, as usual. So, the ending of *sarvavhUtastham* indicates it applies to *Atman* and the translation is therefore: 'the Self, abiding in all beings'.

सर्वभूतानि चात्मनि – *sarvabhUtAni chAtmani*

Here there are four words, *sarva*, *bhUtAni*, *cha* and *Atmani*. This time, *Atmani* is in the seventh case – 'in the Self'. *cha* means 'and, also, moreover etc.' *cha* + *Atmani* = *chAtmani*, in accordance with *akaH savarNe dIrghaH*, the first rule of vowel sandhi given above. *sarvabhUtAni* could have been either nominative or accusative plural. In the context of the sentence, it is clearly the object of the verb 'sees' and translates as: 'and all things (abiding) in the Self'.

योगयुक्तात्मा – *yogayuktAtmA*

This is the subject of the whole sentence. *yogayukta* means 'immersed in deep meditation, absorbed in yoga'. *AtmA* is the nominative singular of *Atman*, used here in the context of the 'individual soul'. Again, *a* + *A* = *A* when the words join.

सर्वत्र समदर्शनः – *sarvatra samadarshanaH*

sarvatra means 'everywhere, at all times'; *sama* means 'like, similar, equal' (our English 'same' clearly derives from it);

darshanaH is the nominative singular masculine of the participle 'seeing, observing, noticing etc.' Again, however, there are not two separate words here. If there were, *sama* would be expected to be in the accusative, being 'what is seen'. In fact, *samadarshanaH* is a single (compound) word, meaning, when used with *sarvatra*, 'looking on all (things or people) with equal or indifferent eyes'. There is a great danger when trying to translate in this way. We try to break up a word into its component parts when, in fact, the whole word itself has a specific meaning and its components do not separate into individually declined words.

The total translation is thus as follows:

In deep meditation, the sage, looking dispassionately on all things, sees the Self abiding in all things, and all things abiding in the Self.

And that should be sufficient to give you the general idea. Internet references are given in the next section for obtaining full details of the rules of *saMdhi* and for downloading your own free digital Monier-Williams, along with pointers to many other resources. With all of these at your disposal and with the knowledge you have now gained, you should be perfectly able to set off on your own path of discovery. To end with, here is a further example for you to practice on, without any clues as to its source or meaning other than to say that it is a sentiment that we would all do well to feel towards our fellows on the planet, whatever spiritual persuasion they may have.

सर्वे भवन्तु सुखिनः सर्वे सन्तु निरामयाः ।
सर्वे भद्राणि पश्यन्तु मा कश्चिद् दुःखभाग्भवेत् ॥

If you really cannot work it out or want to check your answer, the ITRANS and translation are provided in Appendix 5.

Resources on the Internet

A. General Resources

If you intend to utilize what you have learned from this book on your computer in any way, e.g. incorporating Devanagari script into your own documents, then you will need appropriate fonts and tools for generating the script.

The ITRANS scheme was devised by Avinash Chopde. The software, and details about the system, may be downloaded from the website: http://www.aczoom.com/itrans/. It should be noted that the site is no longer maintained or supported. The latest version is 5.32 as of Feb. 2011.

For easy ITRANS representation of Sanskrit, I recommend the use of the excellent software package 'Itranslator 2003', developed by the Sannyasis of Omkarananda Ashram Himalayas, Rishikesh, India. This program, compatible with Windows XP onwards, is freeware, downloadable from

http://www.omkarananda-ashram.org/Sanskrit/Itranslt.html. Words can be typed in ITRANS and converted into Devanagari and Roman diacritical forms. These can then be copied and pasted into any Windows package. This version uses 16-bit Unicode-compatible fonts. Itranslator 99 is still available for 8-bit, non-Unicode, True Type fonts and works with earlier versions of Windows.

Another utility for converting to Devanagari or Romanized transliteration from ITRANS (and vice versa) has been provided from the Argentinian site (see below). This also includes a Monier-Williams Dictionary facility.http://www.sanskrit-sanscrito.com.ar/en/essentials-software-english-home-software-1/697.

http://sanskrit.gde.to/ is one of the main, general sites for Sanskrit-related information. Many documents may be downloaded in a variety of formats: PDF, PS, ITX, GIF, TXT,

Sanskrit98, XDVNG. There are links to dictionaries and grammar-related tools and many exercises relating to conversational Sanskrit. Fonts etc. are available for download and links are provided to ITRANS and postscript tools. Finally, there are links to many other academic and personal Sanskrit-related projects around the world. There are even news broadcasts in Sanskrit, in Real Audio format.

Gerard Huet hosts the 'Sanskrit Heritage Site' site at http://sanskrit.inria.fr/ though many of the resources, including a dictionary with HTML-browser search facilities, are in French-Sanskrit. Many links are provided to other sites.

Finally, my own site has a section devoted to Sanskrit and many resources are listed there – http://www.advaita.org .uk/sanskrit/sanskrit.htm.

B. Learning the Language

As you will certainly have realized quite early in this book, in order to learn how to sound the letters and how correctly to pronounce words, you really need to listen to someone who knows. Since it is unlikely that you will be sufficiently interested to go into it this deeply, however, just follow the instructions and don't worry about how it feels. We are unused to making full use of our mouth and tongue in speaking and, since Sanskrit makes almost scientific use, we will find much of it peculiar and initially uncomfortable. If you want a more thorough introduction to the language, including writing and pronunciation, with little in the way of expense or commitment, there is a truly excellent one available from the Internet. You can download this free of charge and the only cost is the subsequent printing. It is called 'A Practical Sanskrit Introductory' and was produced by Charles Wikner. Numerous versions of it, in different formats, may be downloaded from the site mentioned above – http://sanskritdocuments.org/. This page has dozens of links to related resources for learning – tutorials, grammar, dictionaries etc. I have not looked at most of these so there are doubtless some gems to be found!

The site in Argentina – http://www.sanskrit-sanscrito
.com.ar/en/ – is simply excellent. It takes you from the basics, of
learning to write and pronounce the letters, up to a very comprehensive set of instructions and examples for combining letters
(vowel, visarga and consonant sandhi). There are translations of
Patanjali's Yoga Sutras and other scriptures and audio files of
Sanskrit pronunciation. A tremendous amount of effort has
clearly gone into this project and it shows. It is well presented
and easy to read.

There is a very comprehensive set of online lessons to be
found at http://acharya.iitm.ac.in/sanskrit/lessons/lessons.html.
These were produced between Oct. 1997 and Oct. 2001 by the
Systems Development Laboratory at Chennai, India.
Alternatively, lessons may be downloaded for offline study.
There is also a free multilingual editor, for use in generating web
pages containing Devanagari (and other) scripts. This is needed
in order to be able to make full use of the lessons. [Note that, as
of Feb. 2013, there is a warning that the site is in the process of
being relocated but the resources still seem to be there.]

If you want to go on courses to study the language, there is
the American Sanskrit Institute in Connecticut – see
http://www.americansanskrit.com/. There is a 14-hour weekend
workshop, but I could not find the cost given on the website.
They also offer various courses on CD for home-study. For
example, 'Sanskrit by CD 1 & 2' is $295, as at Feb. 2013.

In the UK, courses are provided by http://www.sanskrit-
courses.co.uk/ in London and Cambridge. There are beginner
and intermediate levels and study for GCSE Sanskrit is also
possible.

Finally, if you are really serious about learning the language,
I have already mentioned the two-volume work by Thomas
Egenes, Ref. 6. Just to repeat, Part 1 is available for free at
http://www.scribd.com/doc/32874508/Introduction-to-Sanskrit-

by-Thomas-Egenes.

C. Dictionaries and Grammar Tools

Gerard Huet's 'Sanskrit Heritage' site, mentioned in the first section, provides an online tool whereby you can specify the stem of a noun (*prAtipadika* form), together with its gender, and it will provide you with a tabular listing of all of the cases. There is also a 'sandhi analysis' utility that will attempt to break a sentence into words. http://sanskrit.inria.fr/. Declensions of nouns and conjugations of verbs can be found at http://sanskrit.inria.fr/DICO/grammar.html.

The University of Cologne has done an incredible job of digitizing much of the Monier-Williams Sanskrit-to-English dictionary. This may be used online at http://www.sanskrit-lexicon.uni-koeln.de/scans/MWScan/tamil/index.html.

However, it may be downloaded in its entirety (19Mb compressed to 7Mb) together with a superb utility for accessing the content. This facility has been provided by Louis Bontes at http://members.chello.nl/l.bontes/. NB: This has not been maintained since 2002 and is only in Beta form – but it works!

D. Documents in Sanskrit

(In addition to sites already mentioned above, which may also contain downloadable documents.)

Bhagavad Gita:
The Sanskrit original, together with verse-by-verse translation into many languages, is available at http://www.bhagavad-gita.org/ (with audio output too if you have the RealPlayer add-on for your browser).

Upanishads:
There are word-by-word translations, together with the original Sanskrit, for a number of the main Upanishads at http://www.

vidyavrikshah.org, although you may have to install some fonts in order to see them. You can download all of the ITRANS for these from http://sanskritdocuments.org/, and convert them to Devanagari using the resources mentioned in Section A.

Chants:
If you would like to hear some Sanskrit being chanted, there are a number of sites which offer such facilities, e.g. http://sanskrit .safire.com/. There are a huge number of documents in PDF format which can be followed while you listen to them being read.

Miscellaneous:
Many additional and other resources, together with any updates or corrections to these links, may be found at my own website – www.advaita.org.uk – under the Sanskrit menu.

Glossary of Sanskrit Terms

Note: A word will normally be given in typical English spelling (non-italic) followed by the ITRANS representation (italic) in brackets, e.g. '**Devanagari (Devanagari)**'. For some definitions, no Sanskrit equivalent is appropriate. In some cases, a word will never be encountered in 'English' form and only the ITRANS representation will be given, e.g. *ach*.

ach – the *pratyAhAra*, from the *maheshvarANi sUtrANi*, used to identify all the vowels.

ach saMdhi – (the rules relating to) the joining of vowels at the end of one word and the beginning of the next. *ach* is the *pratyAhAra* for 'all vowels'.

adhikAra – means 'topic' or 'subject'. The sutras in the *maheshvarANi sUtrANi*, for example, occur within chapters. The main subject is introduced at the beginning. Key words are assumed to apply to sutras in the rest of the chapter and are not repeated. They have to be mentally 'brought down' from the earlier sutras as necessary (*anuvRRitti*).

aghoSha – refers to those letters that make a hard sound in their pronunciation and could not really be regarded as sounding a syllable. (By contrast, letters such as 'b', for example, might be written 'ba' or 'bu' or actually something in between the two). Monier-Williams defines them as 'non-sonant', having 'an absence of all sound or soft murmur'. They are sounded by opening the mouth and allowing the basic *a* sound to emerge, modified as necessary by altering the mouth (tongue, lips) as necessary. The unvoiced or *aghoSha* letters are all the vowels (except for the *visarga*) and the first two rows of the main set of consonants, i.e. *k, ch, T, t, p* and *kh, Ch, Th, th, ph*), plus the sibilants (*sh, Sh, s*). See *ghoSha*, unvoiced, voiced.

akShara – syllable or letter of the alphabet. The word literally means 'imperishable'.

al – the *pratyAhAra*, from the *maheshvarANi sUtrANi*, used to identify all the letters.

Alpaprana (*alpaprANa*) – describes a consonant that is sounded without any additional expelling of air. It means 'with little breath'. Specifically, it is used for those consonants on the first and third rows of the main groups, namely *k, ch, T, t, p* and *g, j, D, d, b*.

Antastha (*antaHstha*) – the Sanskrit term for the 'semi-vowels': *y, r, l, v*. These are formed by combination of *i, RRi, LLi* and *u*, respectively with the vowel *a*. The word literally means 'stand between'.

Anunasika (*anunAsika*) – refers to one of the letters that is sounded 'through the nose', i.e. the last row of the main groups of consonants: *~N, ~n, N, n, m*.

Anusvara (*anusvAra*) – This literally means 'after sound'. It is represented as '*aM*' but is not actually a letter and does not occur on its own. It changes the sound of a letter, causing the associated vowel to be sounded through the nose. In ITRANS, it is represented by *M* or *.n* and in Romanized transliteration by a dot, above or below the preceding consonant. The precise nature of the sound is determined by the consonant that follows. It will take on the sound of the *anunAsika* in the same group as this consonant. E.g. in *saMdhi*, the sound will be that of *n* while in *shaMkara*, it will be that of *~N*.

anuvRRitti – literally means 'the continued course or influence of a preceding rule on what follows'. The sutras in the *maheshvarANi sUtrANi*, for example, occur within chapters. The main subject is introduced at the beginning. Key words are assumed to apply to sutras in the rest of the chapter and are not repeated. They have to be mentally 'brought down' from the earlier sutra as necessary.

Ardachandra (*ardhachandra*) – the concave shape sometimes used in old manuscripts instead of the *anusvAra* but performing the same function. It looks like the *chandra bindu* but without the dot. It means 'crescent-shaped' and can be generated in ITRANS by putting *.c* after the related letter.

Ashtadyayi (*aShTAdhyAyI*) – the classic work on Sanskrit grammar produced by Panini, circa 500 BC.

Avagraha (*avagraha*) – the special symbol used between a word ending in *e* or *o* and one beginning with *a* to indicate that the *a* is not sounded. It is similar to elision in French and is shown in Romanized transliteration by dropping the *a* and inserting an apostrophe, again similar to French. In ITRANS the *a* is left unchanged but a single full stop is inserted instead of the space between the two words.

avyaya – 'indeclinable', applied to those *prAtipadika*-s that do not add *vibhakti* endings.

Ayogavaha (*ayogavAha*) – term for the *anusvAra* and *visarga*, which are not really vowels but are not consonants either. The word means 'not belonging to'. See *yogavAha*.

bahu-vachana – 'plural', with respect to 'number' of nouns or verbs.

chaturthI vibhakti – the fourth, dative case of nouns, i.e. the indirect object, as in 'he gives the letter *to the postman*'.

Cerebral – mouth position used for speaking one of the main groups of letters, the *mUrdhanya* group, with the tongue raised to the roof of the mouth – *RRi, RRI, T, Th, D, Dh, N, r, Sh.*

Chandra-bindu (*chandra bindu*) – the name for the special symbol (shallow, concave bowl, containing a dot) that sometimes appears above a vowel. Its most frequent usage is as part of the special *praNava shabda* symbol for *OM*. The literal meaning is 'moon-like spot' and it indicates that the vowel over which it appears should be sounded through the nose. It is represented in ITRANS by *.N* after the vowel.

chu.N – an abbreviation used to refer to the *halanta* palatal consonants, i.e. *ch, Ch, j, jh* and *~n*. The *.N* inserts a *chandra bindu* above the *chu* and causes the *u* to be sounded through the nose.

Complex vowels – refers to *e, o, ai* and *au*, so-called because they are formed by combining the simple vowels *i* and *u* with *a*. The Sanskrit term is *saMyukta svara*.

Dantya (*dantya*) – mouth position used for speaking one of the main groups of letters, the dental group, with the tongue touching the back of the teeth – *LLi, LLI, t, th, d, dh, n, l, s*.

Dental – mouth position used for speaking one of the main groups of letters, the *dantya* group, with the tongue touching the back of the teeth – *LLi, LLI, t, th, d, dh, n, l, s*.

Devanagari (*devanAgari*) – the name given to the script used for Sanskrit. It means 'city of the gods'.

Dhatu (*dhAtu*) – the 'root' of a word. There are only about two thousand of these and all Sanskrit words are derived from one or more. Words are formed by adding prefix/suffix endings, called *pratyaya*, to form stem-words, called *prAtipadika*. These are the form encountered in the dictionary. They then add the appropriate endings (for nouns and verbs), called *vibhakti*, to form actual 'words', called *pada*.

Diacritic or Diacritical (marks) – the correct name for the special accents used in the Romanized transliteration of Sanskrit. They include lines above some letters and dots above or below others. They are needed because the Sanskrit alphabet has many more than the 26 characters of the English alphabet. See Transliteration.

dIrgha – refers to the *long* vowels: *A, I, RRI, LLI* and *U*, sounding for two 'measures'. The short form is *hrasva*. The complex vowels *e, ai, o* and *au* are necessarily long since they combine other vowel sounds with *a*.

dvitIyA vibhakti – the second, accusative case of nouns, i.e. the direct object, as in 'he opens *the box*'.

dvi-vachana – dual, with respect to 'number' of nouns.

eka-vachana – singular, with respect to 'number' of nouns.

External sandhi (*saMdhi*) – the joining of letters at the end of one word and the beginning of the next.

ghoSha – refers to those letters that could be thought of as sounding a syllable in their pronunciation. The voiced or *ghoSha* letters are all of the consonants except for the first two rows of the main group, plus the *visarga* and semi-vowels. i.e. *g, j, D, d, b; gh, jh, Dh, dh, bh; ~N, ~n, N, n, m; sh, Sh, s, h, H, y, r, l, v*). See *aghoSha*, unvoiced, voiced.

Guna (*guNa*) – term used to refer to the 'stronger' vowels, formed by adding *a* to the simple vowels. *a* remains as *a*, *i* becomes *e*, *u* becomes *o*, *RRi* becomes *ar*, and *LLi* becomes *al*. When a further *a* is added, the *guNa* forms become *vRRiddhi*. This principle becomes important when considering how part-words combine to form words (so-called 'internal *saMdhi*').

Guru (*guru*) – In the context of Sanskrit pronunciation, this is used to refer to a syllable that is stressed. *guru* means 'heavy'. An unstressed syllable is called *laghu*.

Guttural – mouth position used for speaking one of the main groups of letters, the *kaNThya* group, involving the throat – *a, A, k, kh, g, gh, ~N, h*.

hal – the *pratyAhAra*, from the *maheshvarANi sUtrANi*, used to identify all the consonants.

hal saMdhi – (the rules relating to) the joining of consonants at the end of one word and the beginning of the next. *hal* is the *pratyAhAra* for 'all consonants'.

Halanta (*halanta*) – a consonant that is not sounded with a vowel after it. It is marked as such by the use of a *virAma*. The term derives from the *pratyAhAra* '*hal*', which refers to 'any consonant', and *anta*, which means 'end', since such consonants normally occur at the end of a word.

hrasva – refers to the *short* vowels: *a, i, RRi, LLi* and *u*, sounding for one 'measure'. The long form is *dIrgha*.

Internal sandhi (*saMdhi*) – the joining of letters at the end of one part-word and the beginning of the next within a single word.

It (*it*) – the term given to the final, *halanta* letters at the end of each sutra in the *maheshvarANi sUtrANi*. They are used as indicator letters only and are not themselves included in the letters defined by a *pratyAhAra*. The correct term is *it varna*, where *varna* means 'sound or letter'.

ITRANS – the transliterated form of Sanskrit most commonly encountered on the Internet. It uses only those characters that may be typed easily on a computer keyboard so that Sanskrit words can be communicated via email etc. See Transliteration.

jhal – the *pratyAhAra* for 'any consonant other than a nasal or a semi-vowel'.

Kanthya (*kaNThya*) – mouth position used for speaking one of the main groups of letters, the guttural group, involving the throat – *a, A, k, kh, g, gh, ~N, h. kanthah* means 'throat'.

karman – the direct object of the verb in a sentence.

kartRRi – the 'agent' of the verb in a sentence, i.e. 'subject'.

kriyA – the verb in a sentence.

kriyAvibhakti – number and tense endings added to verbs as part of conjugation. Also called *ti~N-vibhakti*.

kriyA-visheShaNa – an adverb.

Labial – mouth position used for speaking one of the main groups of letters, the *oShThya* group, involving the lips – *u, U, p, ph, b, bh, m, v.*

laghu – In the context of Sanskrit pronunciation, this is used to refer to a syllable that is not stressed. *laghu* means 'light'. A stressed syllable is called *guru*.

Lexicographers (L) – the term used in the Sanskrit–English dictionary of Monier-Williams to indicate that the related word has never actually been found in any scriptural or historical text and is really only of academic interest (to those who compile dictionaries).

li~Nga – gender of nouns.

madhyama-puruSha – 'middle person' of verbs – equivalent to English second person, i.e. 'you'.

Mahaprana (*mahAprANa*) – describes a consonant that is

sounded with additional expelling of air. It means 'with much breath'. Specifically, it is used for those consonants on the second and fourth rows of the main groups, namely *kh, Ch, Th, th, ph* and *gh, jh, Dh, dh, bh*.

Maheshvarani Sutrani (*maheshvarANi sUtrANi*) – a set of 14 sutras, each of which is actually just a group of letters from the alphabet. The shorthand term of a single letter, together with one of the letters at the end of one of the 14 groups, is then used to specify all of the letters (excluding group terminating letters, which are called *it*) between those two. In this way, collections of letters with specific properties may be defined e.g. all consonants, all semi-vowels etc. The combination of two letters used for this purpose is called a *pratyAhAra*. The system was defined by Panini about two and a half thousand years ago. *maheshvara* means 'great lord'.

mAtrA – 'measure', in respect of the length of a vowel. Short (*hrasva*) vowels such as *a* are sounded for one *mAtrA*, long (*dIrgha*) for two *mAtrA*, and *pluta* vowels for three or more.

mAtRRikA – the name given to all of the vowel sounds plus the *anusvAra* and *visarga*: *a, A, i, I, RRi, RRI, LLi, LLI, u, U, e, o, ai, au, aM, aH*. The word literally means 'divine mothers' but is used in the sense of written characters that have magical powers.

mUrdhanya – mouth position used for speaking one of the main groups of letters, the cerebral group, with the tongue raised to the roof of the mouth – *RRi, RRI, T, Th, D, Dh, N, r, Sh*.

nAman – a noun.

nAma-vibhakti – number, gender and case endings added to nouns and adjectives; also called *sup-vibhakti*.

napuMsaka-li~Nga – neuter gender of nouns.

oShThya – mouth position used for speaking one of the main groups of letters, the labial group, involving the lips – *u, U, p, ph, b, bh, m, v*.

Pada (*pada*) – the term for a word that has added all necessary endings for nouns/verbs, so that it can be used without further alteration in a sentence. See *dhAtu, prAtipadika*.

Palatal – mouth position used for speaking one of the main groups of letters, the *tAlavya* group, with the back of the tongue raised to the roof of the mouth – *i, I, ch, Ch, j, jh, ~n, y, sh*.

pa~nchami vibhakti – the fifth, ablative case of nouns, indicating 'from' or 'out of' etc., e.g. she walks *from the house*.

Panini (*pANini*) – the Sanskrit grammarian, circa 500 BC, who collated all of the rules for sandhi and grammar in a book called the *aShTAdhyAyI*.

parasmaipada – active voice of verbs.

pluta – refers to a prolonged vowel (i.e. longer than the two measures of *dIrgha*). It is represented by writing the (Sanskrit) number '3' below right or immediately after the letter to be sounded prolonged.

Pranava shabda (*praNava shabda*) – term for the special symbol for the mystical word *OM*.

prathama-puruSha – 'first person' of verbs – equivalent to English third person, i.e. 'he, she or it'.

prathamA vibhakti – first, nominative case of nouns, i.e. the subject of a sentence.

prAtipadika – the 'stem-form' of words, as found in the dictionary, i.e. without endings for gender, number, case, tense etc. See *dhAtu*.

Pratyahara (*pratyAhAra*) – the term given to the two-letter (single syllable), shorthand identifier used to define a group of letters in the *maheshvarANi sUtrANi*. (The same technique is also used elsewhere and is given the same name.)

pratyaya – prefixes or suffixes, added to a *dhAtu*, to form a *prAtipadika*.

puM-li~Nga – masculine gender of nouns.

Purnavirama (*pUrNavirAma*) – the double vertical line used to mark the end of a paragraph or verse of a *sUtra*. It is generated in ITRANS by two full stops or two 'shift + \'.

puruSha – 'person' in respect of verb-endings.

Romanized – the transliterated form of Sanskrit most commonly encountered in books and, for example, PDF (portable document format) files downloaded from the Internet. It uses the 'English' alphabet together with 'diacritical marks' or accents such as dots above or below letters. See Transliteration.

samAsa – a compound word. The word literally means 'placed together'.

saMbodhana – vocative case of nouns. Nouns are generally regarded as having seven case endings but this is effectively the eighth. It is used when addressing someone directly, e.g. *'Boy, come over here!'*

saMhitA – Panini's alternative word for sandhi. It is defined as 'the closest drawing together of sounds'.

saMj~na – a proper noun.

Samyoga (*saMyoga*) – term for a conjunct consonant, i.e. two or more consonants joined together without an intervening vowel sound. The word literally means 'joined together'.

Samyukta svara (*saMyukta svara*) – term for the complex vowels, *e, o, ai, au*. *saMyukta* means 'joined together' or 'combined'.

Sandhi (*saMdhi*) – a comprehensive set of rules governing the way in which sounds combine when they appear next to each other. These prevent, for example, the situation where one word ends in a vowel and the next word begins with one, by merging the two. There are three 'classes' of sandhi: vowel, consonant, and *visarga*.

saptamI vibhakti – seventh, locative case of nouns, referring to the time or place where the action takes place, e.g. they ate their picnic *on the lawn*.

sarva-nAman – a pronoun. The word literally means 'name of all'.

ShaShThI vibhakti – sixth, genitive case of nouns e.g. the *dog's* bone (the bone *belonging to the dog*).

Savarna (*savarNa*) – refers to a 'similar sound' in the context of sandhi. The word literally means 'of the same family'. E.g. *a* and *A* are *savarNa*.

Shakti (*shakti*) – another name (see *mAtRRikA*) given to all of the vowel sounds plus the *anusvAra* and *visarga*: *a, A, i, I, RRi, RRI, LLi, LLI, u, U, e, o, ai, au, aM, aH*. The word literally means 'power' or 'strength'.

shar – the *pratyAhAra*, from the *maheshvarANi sUtrANi*, used to identify the sibilants.

Sibilant – refers to the 'ss' sounds *sh, Sh* and *s*. The Sanskrit term is *UShman*, though this also includes the letter *h*.

Sparsha (*sparsha*) – term for the 25 consonants, i.e. excluding semi-vowels, sibilants and *h*. The term literally means 'touching' or 'contact' and refers to the fact that the underlying vowel sound is modified by contact in the mouth in such a way as to 'stop' it in some way.

strI-li~Nga – feminine gender of nouns.

sup-vibhakti – number, gender and case endings added to nouns and adjectives; also called *namavibhakti*. *sup* is a *pratyAhAra*.

Svara (*svara*) – Sanskrit term for a vowel, literally meaning 'sound'.

tAlavya – mouth position used for speaking one of the main groups of letters, the palatal group, with the back of the tongue raised to the roof of the mouth – *i, I, ch, Ch, j, jh, ~n, y, sh*.

ti~N-vibhakti – number and tense endings added to verbs as part of conjugation. Also called *kriyAvibhakti*. *ti~N* is a *pratyAhAra*.

Transliteration – a representation of the Sanskrit alphabet using letters of the English alphabet, together with other special characters. See Romanized, ITRANS.

tRRitIyA vibhakti – the third or instrumental case of nouns, e.g. 'he writes *with a pen*' or 'she travels *by bus*'.

tu.N – an abbreviation used to refer to the *halanta* dental consonants, i.e. *t, th, d, dh* and *n*. The *.N* inserts a *chandra bindu* above the *tu* and causes the *u* to be sounded through the nose.

Unvoiced – refers to those letters that do not sound like a syllable in their pronunciation. A hard, clipped sound is made by opening the mouth and allowing the basic *a* sound to emerge, modified by altering the mouth (tongue, lips) as necessary. The unvoiced or *aghoSha* letters are all the vowels (except for the *visarga*) and the first two rows of the main set of consonants, i.e. *k, ch, T, t, p* and *kh, Ch, Th, th, ph*), plus the sibilants (*sh, Sh, s*). See *aghoSha, ghoSha,* voiced.

Upasarga (*upasarga*) – a preposition. Often occurs as a prefix to a verb and is separable.

Ushman (*UShman*) – the Sanskrit term for the sibilants, *sh, Sh* and *s,* together with *h.* The word itself literally means 'heat, steam or vapor'.

uttama-puruSha – 'last person' of verbs – equivalent to English first person, i.e. 'I'.

vachana – number of a noun, singular, dual or plural.

Vedic *anusvAra* – the symbol of a *chandra bindu* together with a *virAma* appearing at the end of a word but not over/under a specific letter. It means that the preceding word is not pronounced in the usual way but in so-called 'Vedic pronunci-ation', presumably in order to satisfy metrical requirements of the poetry. See example in Level 2 Section H.

Vibhakti (*vibhakti*) – number, gender and case endings added to nouns and adjectives are called *namavibhakti* or *sup-vibhakti.* Similarly, verb endings for tense and number are called *kriyAvibhakti* or *ti~N-vibhakti.* Only when all such endings have been added to a *prAtipadika* do we get a 'word' or *pada.*

Virama (*virAma*) – the diagonal mark underneath a consonant to indicate that it is not to be sounded with a vowel after it. The literal meaning is 'cessation, termination or end'. {All consonants are sounded with 'a' by default, unless indicated otherwise.} A consonant with such a mark is called an *halanta* consonant.

OR – the single vertical mark to indicate the end of a sentence or single line of a verse of poetry.

Visarga (*visarga*) – this literally means 'sending out' or 'emission'. It is represented as '*aH*' but is not actually a letter and does not occur on its own. Its effect is to add a brief, breathing out sound after the vowel sound associated with a consonant. It is represented by two dots placed to the right of the associated letter.

visheShaNa – adjective.

Voiced – refers to those letters that make a syllable in their pronunciation; a soft 'murmuring' sound unlike the hard, clipped sound of the unvoiced letters. The voiced or *ghoSha* letters are all of the consonants except for the first two rows of the main group, plus the *visarga* and semi-vowels. i.e. *g, j, D, d, b; gh, jh, Dh, dh, bh; ~N, ~n, N, n, m; sh, Sh, s, h, H, y, r, l, v*). See *aghoSha*, *ghoSha*, unvoiced.

Vriddhi (*vRRiddhi*) – term used to refer to the 'strongest' vowel sounds, when *a* has been added a second time to the simple vowels. (When *a* has been added once, the *guNa* form results.) The *vRRiddhi* form of *a* is *A*, of *i* is *ai*, of *u* is *au*, of *RRi* is *Ar* and of *LLi* is *Al*. This principle becomes important when considering how part-words combine to form words (so-called 'internal *saMdhi*').

Vyanjana (*vya~njana*) – Sanskrit term for a consonant, meaning a 'decoration' (of the basic vowel sound).

yaN – the *pratyAhAra*, from the *maheshvarANi sUtrANi*, used to identify the semi-vowels.

yar – the *pratyAhAra* for all the consonants except *h*.

Yogavaha (*yogavAha*) – term for the *anusvAra* and *visarga*, which are not really vowels but are not consonants either. The word means 'belonging to', since they need another 'real' letter in order to have any meaning. See *ayogavAha*.

Dictionary of Common Sanskrit
Spiritual Words

[Each word is given in the following format:

Typical English Spelling (*ITRANS representation*, Devanagari Script) – meaning

(Words appear in order of the English (Roman) alphabet, not the Sanskrit alphabet.)]

a (*a*, अ) – as a prefix to another word, it changes it into the negative. e.g. *vidya* – knowledge, *avidya* – ignorance.

abhidharma (*abhidharma*, अभिधर्म) – the metaphysical scriptures of Buddhist philosophy.

acharya (*AchArya*, आचार्य) – a spiritual guide or teacher. See Shankaracharya.

achintya (*achintya*, अचिन्त्य) – inconceivable or beyond thought.

adhyaropa (*adhyAropa*, अध्यारोप) – erroneously attributing one thing to another.

adhyasa (*adhyAsa*, अध्यास) – used to refer to the 'mistake' that we make when we 'superimpose' a false appearance upon the reality or mix up the real and the unreal. The classical example is when we see a snake instead of a rope, which is used as a metaphor for seeing the world of objects instead of the reality of the Self. This concept is fundamental to Advaita and Shankara devotes a separate section to it at the beginning of his commentary on the Brahmasutra.

Advaita (*advaita*, अद्वैत) – not (*a*) two (*dvaita*); non-dual philosophy.

agamin (*AgAmin*, आगामिन्) – that type of sanskara which is generated in reaction to current situations and which will not bear fruit until sometime in the future. It literally means 'impending', 'approaching' or 'coming'. Also called *kriyamANa*, which means 'being done'. See prarabdha, sanchita, sanskara.

aham (*aham,* अहम्) – I am.

aham vritti (*aham vRRitti,* अहम् वृत्ति) – the thought 'I am' as opposed to thoughts about objects, feelings etc. – idam vritti. See vritti.

ahankara (*ahaMkAra,* अहंकार) – the making, kara (*kAra*), of the utterance 'I', aham (*aham*); this is the equivalent of what we would call the 'ego' but specifically refers to the identification or attachment of our true Self with something else, usually the body or mind but can be much more specific e.g. I am a teacher, I am a woman. It is one of the 'organs' of the mind in classical Advaita – see antakarana.

ajati (*ajAti,* अजाति) – *a* – no or not; *jAti* – creation; the principle that the world and everything in it, including these mind-body appearances, were never created or 'brought into existence'. Most clearly stated by Gaudapada in his karika on the Mandukya Upanishad.

ajnana (*aj~nAna,* अज्ञान) – (spiritual) ignorance. See jnana.

anadi (*anAdi,* अनादि) – without any beginning, often used to describe 'ignorance'.

ananda (*Ananda,* आनन्द) – 'true' happiness; usually called 'bliss' to differentiate it from the transient variety that always alternates with pain or misery. It is an aspect of our true nature and is often combined with the other elements of our real nature – sat and chit – into a single word, satchidananda. See sat, chit and satchidananda.

anatman (*anAtman,* अनात्मन्) – something other than spirit or soul (not Self or atman); perceptible world. See atman.

anirvachaniya (*anirvachanIya,* अनिर्वचनीय) – unutterable, indescribable, not to be mentioned. Used to 'describe' the nature of reality etc.

anitya (*anitya,* अनित्य) – transient. Also **anityatva** (*anityatva,* अनित्यत्व) – transient or limited existence (mortality).

anta (*anta,* अन्त) – end, conclusion, death etc.

antakarana (*antaHkaraNa,* अन्तःकरण) – used to refer to the overall 'organ' of mind; the seat of thought and feeling. It consists of a number of separate functions – see manas, buddhi, chitta and ahankara.

anubhava (*anubhava,* अनुभव) – perception, understanding, experience; knowledge derived from personal observation.

anumana (*anumAna,* अनुमान) – inference (in logic); one of the six means of obtaining knowledge. See pramana.

anupalabdhi (*anupalabdhi,* अनुपलब्धि) – non-perception, non-recognition; one of the six means of obtaining knowledge. See pramana.

apaurusheya (*apauruSheya,* अपौरुषेय) – literally 'not coming from human beings'; used to refer to the shruti – scriptural texts passed on verbatim from generation to generation since their original observation by realized sages. See shruti.

artha (*artha,* अर्थ) – acquisition of wealth. See purushartha.

arthapatti (*arthApatti,* अर्थापत्ति) – inference from circumstances, presumption; one of the six means of obtaining knowledge. See pramana.

asat (asat, असत्) – non-existent. See sat.

asparsha (*asparsha,* अस्पर्श) – intangible, 'touchless'; name given to the 'contentless' yoga of Gaudapada in the Mandukya Upanishad.

Astavakra (*aShTAvakra,* अष्टावक्र) – the eponymous Sage of the Astavakra Gita (or Samhita). The word literally means 'twisted' (*vakra*) in 'eight' (*aShTan*) ways. Astavakra was so called because he was born severely deformed after being cursed in the womb by his father (because the unborn child had criticized him for making mistakes while reading the scriptures!). (Later in life, after he had secured his father's release through defeating the court philosopher in debate, his father blessed him and, after swimming in a sacred river, he was cured.) See gita, samhita.

astika (*Astika,* आस्तिक) – literally 'there is or exists'; used to refer to one who believes in the existence of God or, more specifically, one who defers to the authority of the Vedas. See nastika, veda.

atma (*Atma,* आत्म) – see atman.

atmabodha (*Atmabodha,* आत्मबोध) – knowledge of Self; a book attributed to Shankara.

atman (*Atman,* आत्मन्) – the Self. Usually used to refer to one's true (individual) nature or consciousness but Advaita tells us that there is no such thing as an 'individual' and that this atman is the same as the universal Consciousness, Brahman. See also jiva.

atmavicara (*AtmavichAra,* आत्मविचार) – *vicAra* in this context means reflection or examination; upon the *Atman,* the Self. See atman.

avacheda-vada (*avachCheda-vAda,* अवच्छेद वाद) – theory that the Self is limited by ignorance in the forms of upadhis. See upadhi.

avarana (*AvaraNa,* आवरण) – the 'veiling' power of maya. In the rope–snake metaphor, this power prevents us from seeing the reality of the rope. See maya, vikshepa.

avidya (*avidyA,* अविद्या) – ignorance (in a spiritual sense) i.e. that which prevents us from realizing the Self. See also maya.

avrita (*AvRRita,* आवृत) – covered or concealed.

badha (*bAdha,* बाध) – sublation or subration. This is the process by which an accepted point of view or understanding is superseded by a totally different one when some new information is received. An example is seeing a lake in the desert and then realizing that it is only a mirage.

bandha or bandhana (*bandha* or *bandhana,* बन्ध or बन्धन) – bondage, attachment to the world.

bauddha (*bauddha,* बौद्ध) – in the mind, related to the intellect; related to (the teaching of) Buddha.

Bhagavad (*bhagavad,* भगवद्) – in the context of Bhagavad Gita (on its own, the *d* would change to a *t*) it refers to the god Krishna, and Bhagavad Gita means Krishna's Song. (Bhagavat means 'prosperous, happy' etc.) See gita.

Bhagavad Gita (*bhagavadgItA,* भगवद्गीता) – the scriptural text forming part of the Hindu epic, the Mahabarata. It is a dialogue between Krishna, the charioteer/God, and .the warrior Arjuna, representing you and me, on the battlefield of Kurukshetra prior to the commencement of battle. The scripture is regarded as smriti. See Bhagavad, smriti.

bhakta (*bhakta,* भक्त) – one who practices bhakti yoga. See bhakti yoga.

bhakti (*bhakti,* भक्ति) yoga – devotion or worship. See also karma and jnana.

bhashya (*bhAShya,* भाष्य) – explanatory work, exposition or commentary on some other scriptural document. Thus Shankara, for example, has written bhashyas on a number of Upanishads, the Bhagavad Gita and the Brahmasutra.

bhava (*bhAva,* भाव) – condition or state of body or mind; continuity of the thread of existence through successive births (Buddhism)

bhoktri (*bhoktRRi,* भोक्तृ) – one who enjoys; an 'experiencer' or 'feeler'.

Brahma (*brahma,* ब्रह्म) – God as the creator of the universe in Hindu mythology (the others are Vishnu, *viShNu,* the preserver and Shiva, *shiva,* the destroyer). NB: Not to be confused with Brahman!

brahmacharya (*brahmacharya,* ब्रह्मचर्य) – the first stage of the traditional Hindu spiritual path, in which the Brahmin begins his life as an unmarried, religious and chaste student. (*charya* means 'due observance of all rites and customs'.) See also grihasta, sanyasa, vanaprastha.

Brahman (*brahman,* ब्रह्मन्) – the universal Self, Absolute or God. There is only Brahman. It derives from the Sanskrit root *bRRih,* meaning to grow great or strong, and could be thought of as the adjective 'big' made into a noun, implying that which is greater than anything. See also atman, Brahma, jiva, jivatman, paramatman.

Brahma Sutra (*brahmasUtra,* ब्रह्मसूत्र) – a book (in sutra form, which is terse verse!) by Vyasa. This book is the best known of the third accepted source of knowledge (nyaya prasthana). Effectively, it attempts to summarize the Upanishads. It has been extensively commented on by the three main schools of Vedanta philosophy: dvaita, advaita and vishishtadvaita, and the proponents of each claim that it substantiates their beliefs. Shankara has commented on it and provided extensive arguments against any interpretation other than that of Advaita. See bhashya, nyaya prasthana, sruti, smriti.

brahmavidya (*brahmavidyA,* ब्रह्मविद्या) – knowledge of the one Self . See brahman.

Brihadaranyaka (*bRRihadAraNyaka,* बृहदारण्यक) – one of the major Upanishads (and possibly the oldest). See Upanishad.

buddhi (*buddhi,* बुद्धि) – the organ of mind responsible for discrimination and judgment, perhaps nearest equated to the intellect in Western usage. See also, ahankara, antakarana, manas and chitta.

chakra (*chakra,* चक्र) – literally 'circle' or 'wheel'; one of the points in the spine through which energy is supposed to flow in kundalini yoga.

chatushtaya sampatti (*chatuShTaya sampatti,* चतुष्टय सम्पत्ति) – the fourfold prerequisites specified by Shankara as needed by a seeker before he or she can successfully seek Self-knowledge. *chatuShTaya* means 'fourfold'; *sampatti* means 'success' or 'accomplishment'. See sadhana, vairagya, viveka, mumukshutvam.

chetana (*chetana,* चेतन) – consciousness, intelligence etc.

chit (*chit,* चित्) – pure thought or Consciousness. See ananda, sat, satchidananda.

chitta (*chitta,* चित्त) – the organ (part) of mind responsible for memory. See antakarana, ahankara, buddhi, manas.

dama (*dama,* दम) – self-restraint but understood as control over the senses; one of the 'six qualities' that form part of Shankara's chatushtaya sampatti. See chatushtaya sampatti.

darshana (*darshana,* दर्शन) – audience or meeting (with a guru); viewpoint; system of philosophy (the six classical Indian philosophical systems are: purvamimamsa, uttaramimamsa, nyaya, vaisheshika, Sankhya, yoga).

dehatmavada (*dehAtmavAda,* देहात्मवाद) – materialism.

deha, (*deha,* देह) – person, individual, outward form or appearance (body).

dharma (*dharma,* धर्म) – customary practice, conduct, duty, justice and morality. The favored meaning of most traditional teachers is, however, 'nature, character, essential quality', which they often translate as 'essence'. Our own dharma (*svadharma*) is what we ought to do with our lives in order to dissolve our accumulation of sanskara. See sanskara, karma.

drishtanta (*dRRiShTAnta,* दृष्टान्त) – 'the end or aim of what is seen', example or instance.

drishti-srishti-vada (*dRRiShTisRRiShTivAda,* दृष्टिसृष्टिवाद) – the theory that our mistaken view of the world arises from a mental image (based on memory and sense data) superimposed upon the reality. *dRRiShTi* means 'seeing'; *sRRiShTi* means 'creation'; *vAda* means 'thesis' or 'doctrine'. See also adhyasa, ajati, srishti-drishti-vada.

dukha (*duHkha,* दुःख) – pain, sorrow, trouble.

dvaita (*dvaita,* द्वैत) – duality, philosophy of dualism; belief that God and the atman are separate entities. Madhva is the scholar most often associated with this philosophy.

Gaudapada (*gauDapAda,* गौडपाद) – the author of the commentary (karika) on the Mandukya Upanishad. He is said to have been the teacher of Shankara's teacher. See karika, Mandukya, Upanishad.

gita (*gItA,* गीता) – a sacred song or poem but more usually refers to philosophical or religious doctrines in verse form (*gIta* means 'sung'). The most famous are the Bhagavad Gita and

Astavakra Gita. If the word is used on its own, it will be referring to the former. See Bhagavad, Astavakra.

grihasta (*gRRihastha*, गृहस्थ) – this is the second stage of the traditional Hindu spiritual path, called the period of the 'householder', in which the Brahmin performs the duties of master of the house and father of a family. See also brahmacharya, grihasta, sanyasa, vanaprastha.

guna (*guNa*, गुण) – according to classical Advaita, creation can be said to be describable by three 'attributes': sattva, rajas and tamas. Everything – matter, thoughts, feelings – can be described as a mixture of these three in varying degrees and it is the relative proportions that determine the nature of the thing in question. In Sankhya philosophy, these are actual substances, together constituting the total *prakRRiti* or *pradhAna* that makes up the material universe. See sattwa, rajas and tamas for more details.

guru (*guru*, गुरु) – literally 'heavy'; used to refer to one's elders or a person of reverence but more commonly in the West to indicate one's spiritual teacher.

hetu (*hetu*, हेतु) – cause or reason; the logical reason or argument in a syllogism.

idam vritti (*idam vRRitti*, इदम् वृत्ति) – thoughts of objects, concepts, feelings etc., as opposed to aham vritti – the thought 'I am'. See vritti.

Ishvara (*Ishvara*, ईश्वर) – the Lord; efficient and material cause of the phenomenal universe. See saguna Brahman.

jagat (*jagat*, जगत्) – the world (earth), humankind etc.

jagrat (*jAgrat*, जाग्रत्) – the waking state of consciousness. The 'waker ego' is called vishva. See also sushupti, svapna turiya.

japa (*japa*, जप) – the simple repetition of a mantra; usually associated with the initial stage of meditation. See mantra.

jiva (*jIva*, जीव) – the identification of the atman with a body and mind; 'reflection' of the atman in the mind (*chidAbhAsa*).

See atman.

jivatman (*jIvAtman*, जीवात्मन्) – another word for atman, to emphasize that we are referring to the atman in this embodied state, as opposed to the paramatman, the 'supreme Self'. See atman.

jnana (j~*nAna*, ज्ञान) yoga – yoga based on the acquisition of true knowledge (j~nAna means 'knowledge') i.e. knowledge of the Self as opposed to mere information about the world of appearances. *j~nAna yoga* is the process of *shravaNa, manana* and *nididhyAsana* as part of Self-inquiry. See also bhakti, karma, shravana, manana, nididhyasana.

jnani or jnanin (*j~nAnI* or *j~nAnin*, ज्ञानी or ज्ञानिन्) – one who has attained Self-knowledge (enlightenment) as a result of practicing jnana yoga. (*j~nAnin* is the *prAtipadika*; *j~nAnI* is the nominative singular *pada*.) See jnana yoga.

kali yuga (*kali yuga*, कलि युग)– the present age (Iron age) in the cycle of creation. See kalpa.

kalpa (*kalpa*, कल्प) – one 'day' in the life of Brahma, the Creator; equal to 994 cycles of ages and 4,320,000,000 years (if you're really interested).

kama (*kAma*, काम) – desire, longing. Not to be confused with karma. See purushartha.

kanda (*kANDa*, काण्ड) – part or section, division of a work or book, especially relating to the Vedas.

karika (*kArikA*, कारिका) – (strictly speaking) a concise philosophical statement in verse. The best known is that by Gaudapada on the Mandukya Upanishad. (Not to be confused with *karika*, which is an elephant!) See Gaudapada, Mandukya, Upanishad.

karma (*karma*, कर्म) – literally 'action' but generally used to refer to the 'law' whereby actions carried out now will have their lawful effects in the future (and this may be in future lives). Note that karma yoga is something different – see below. See also sanskara.

karmakanda (*karmakANDa*, कर्मकाण्ड) – that portion of the

Vedas relating to ceremonial acts, the rituals we should follow, sacrificial rites and so on.

karma yoga (*karma yoga,* कर्म योग) – the practice of acting in such a way as not to incur karma, by carrying out 'right' actions, not 'good' or 'bad' ones. See bhakti, karma, jnana.

kartri (*kartRRi,* कर्तृ) – one who makes, does or acts; the agent of an action.

Katha Upanishad (*kaThopaniShad,* कठोपनिषद्) – one of the 108+ Upanishads and one of the ten major ones. *kaTha* was a sage and founder of a branch of the Yajur Veda. See Upanishad.

Kena Upanishad (*kenopaniShad,* केनोपनिषद्) – one of the 108+ Upanishads and another one of the ten major ones. *kena* means 'whence?' ('how?', 'why?' etc.) and is the first word of this Upanishad. See Upanishad.

kosha (*kosha,* कोश) – literally 'sheath' as in the scabbard of a sword; one of the five layers of identification that 'cover up' our true nature.

lakshana (*lakShaNa,* लक्षण) – indicating or expressing indirectly; accurate description or definition.

laukika (*laukika,* लौकिक) – worldly, belonging to or occurring in ordinary life. *laukika anumAna* is inference by scientific reasoning, based on observation.

laya (*laya,* लय) – literally 'dissolution' (and the last stage in the cycle of creation, preservation and destruction of the universe). It is also used to refer to the four-stage process for dissolving ignorance described in the Astavakra Gita. See Astavakra, Gita.

lila (*lIlA,* लीला) – literally 'play', 'amusement' or 'pastime'; the idea that the apparent creation is a diversion for a creator – a means for Him to enjoy Himself. He plays all the parts in such a way that they are ignorant of their real nature and believe themselves separate.

loka (*loka,* लोक) – world, universe, sky or heaven etc.

madhyama (*mAdhyama,* माध्यम) – relating to the middle;

central (*mAdhyamika* is one of the principal schools of Buddhism.)

mahavakyas (*mahAvAkya,* महावाक्य) – *maha* means 'great'; *vAkya* means 'speech, saying or statement'. The four 'great sayings' from the Vedas are: 'Consciousness is Brahman', 'That thou art', 'This Self is Brahman' and 'I am Brahman'.

manana (*manana,* मनन) – reflecting upon what has been heard (shravana). This is the second stage of the classical spiritual path, to remove any doubts about the knowledge that has been received via shravana. See also jnana yoga, samshaya, shravana, nididhyasana.

manas (*manas,* मनस्) – the 'organ' of mind acting as intermediary between the senses and the intellect (buddhi) on the way in and the intellect and the organs of action on the way out. These are its primary functions, and 'thinking' ought to consist only of the processing of data on behalf of the intellect. Unfortunately, it usually tries to take on the role of the intellect itself and this is when thinking becomes a problem. See ahankara, antakarana, buddhi and chitta.

Mandukya (*mANDUkya,* माण्डूक्य) – one of the major Upanishads and possibly the single most important, when considered in conjunction with the karika written by Gaudapada. See Gaudapada, karika, Upanishad.

mantra (*mantra,* मन्त्र) – a group of words (or sometimes only one or more syllables), traditionally having some mystical significance, being in many religions an actual 'name of God'. Often used in meditation (always in Transcendental Meditation). See japa.

maya (*mAyA,* माया) – literally 'magic' or 'witchcraft', often personified in Hindu mythology. The 'force' used to 'explain' how it is that we come to be deceived into believing that there is a creation with separate objects and living creatures etc. See also avarana and vikshepa.

mayakara (*mAyAkAra,* मायाकार) – a maker of magic i.e. a conjurer or magician. See maya.

mimamsa (*mImAMsA,* मीमांसा) – profound thought, reflection, examination. See purvamimamsa, utteramimamsa.

mithya (*mithyA,* मिथ्या) – literally 'incorrectly' or 'improperly'. Ascribed to objects etc., meaning that these are not altogether unreal but not strictly real either i.e. they are our imposition of name and form upon the undifferentiated Self. See adhyasa.

moksha (*moksha,* मोक्ष) – liberation, enlightenment, Self-realization.

mukti (*mukti,* मुक्ति) – setting or becoming free, final liberation.

mumukshutvam (*mumukshutvaM,* मुमुक्षुत्वं) – the desire to achieve enlightenment, to the exclusion of all other desires. See sadhana, chatushtaya sampatti.

Mundaka Upanishad (*muNDakopaniShad,* मुण्डकोपनिषद्) – another one of the 108+ Upanishads and also one of the ten major ones – but not to be confused with the Mandukya. *muNDa* means 'having a shaved head' and the Upanishad is so called because everyone who comprehends its sacred doctrine is 'shorn', i.e. liberated from all error. See Upanishad.

nama-rupa (*nAma-rUpa,* नामरूप) – name and form.

nastika (*nAstika,* नास्तिक) – atheist, unbeliever; strictly speaking, refers to one who does not recognize the authority of the Vedas.

neti (*neti,* नेति) – not this (*na* – not; *iti* – this). From the Brihadaranyaka Upanishad (2.3.6). Used by the intellect whenever it is thought that the Self might be some 'thing' observed e.g. body, mind etc. The Self cannot be anything that is seen, thought or known. See Brihadaranyaka, Upanishad.

nididhyasana (*nididhyAsana,* निदिध्यासन) – meditating upon the essence of what has now been intellectually understood until there is total conviction. The third stage of the classical spiritual path. See also shravana and manana.

nidra (*nidrA,* निद्रा) – sleep.

nirguna (*nirguNa,* निर्गुण) – 'without qualities'; usually referring to Brahman and meaning that it is beyond any description or thought. Since there is only Brahman, any word would imply limitation or duality. See Brahman, saguna, Isvara.

nirvikalpa (*nirvikalpa,* निर्विकल्प) – (referring to samadhi) 'without' division – not seeing the world as separate or different from oneself. See savikalpa, samadhi, vikalpa.

nirvishesha (*nirvisheSha,* निर्विशेष) – making or showing no difference. *nirvisheShaNa* – attributeless.

niyama (*niyama,* नियम) – restraining, controlling; any fixed rule or law; necessity.

nyaya (*nyAya,* न्याय) – literally, 'that into which a thing goes back', a 'standard' or 'rule'; one of the six classical Indian philosophical systems, whose principal exponent was Gautama in the third century BC. It is so called because the system examines all physical and metaphysical subjects in a very logical manner.

nyaya prasthana (*nyAya prasthAna,* न्याय प्रस्थान) – refers to logical and inferential material based upon the Vedas, of which the best known is the Brahmasutra of Vyasa (*nyAya* can also mean 'method', 'axiom', 'logical argument' etc.). See pramana, prasthana-traya, smriti, sruti.

Panchadashi (*pa~nchadashI,* पञ्चदशी) – literally means 'fifteen' because it has this many chapters – a book written by Vidyaranya (*vidyAraNya*), based upon the Upanishads. It discusses many Advaitic truths and uses some original metaphors to illustrate the concepts.

pandita (*paNDita,* पण्डित) – literally 'wise' (as an adjective) or 'scholar, teacher, philosopher' (as a noun) and used in this way in the scriptures.

papa (*pApa,* पाप) – literally 'bad' or 'wicked' but used in the sense of the 'sin' that accrues (according to the theory of karma) from performing 'bad' actions, i.e. those done with a selfish motive. See also punya.

paramatman (*paramAtman,* परमात्मन्) – the 'supreme Self' as opposed to the atman in the 'embodied' state, the jivatman. See atman.

paramartha (noun), (*paramArtha,* परमार्थ);

paramarthika (adj.), (*pAramArthika* (adj.), पारमार्थिक) – the highest truth or reality; the noumenal as opposed to the phenomenal world of appearances (vyavaharika). See pratibhasika and vyavaharika.

parampara (*paramparA,* परम्परा) – literally 'proceeding from one to another'; 'guru parampara' refers to the tradition of guru–disciple passing on wisdom through the ages. See also sampradaya.

phala (*phala,* फल) – fruit; often used in the context of the consequences that necessarily follow as a result of action (*karmaphala*).

prajna (*praj~nA,* प्रज्ञा) – (verb) to know or understand, find out, perceive or learn; (noun) wisdom, intelligence, knowledge. Not to be confused with *prAj~na* below.

prajna (*prAj~na,* प्राज्ञ) – the 'deep sleep ego' in the deep sleep state of consciousness, sushupti. Literally, 'wise, clever' (adj.) or 'a wise person' or 'intelligence dependent on individuality'. See also vishva, taijasa.

prajnana (*praj~nAna,* प्रज्ञान) – consciousness.

pralaya (*pralaya,* प्रलय) – the destruction of the world at the end of a kalpa. See kalpa.

prakarana (*prakaraNa,* प्रकरण) – subject, topic, treatise etc. but especially opening chapter or prologue.

prakriti (*prakRRiti,* प्रकृति) – literally the original or natural form or condition of anything; generally used to refer to what we would call 'nature'. In Sankhya philosophy, it is one of the two principles – *puruSha* and *prakRRiti* (or *pradhAna*) – and is an actually existent, though not conscious thing. In Advaita, it is *mithyA*.

pramana (*pramANa,* प्रमाण) – valid means for acquiring

knowledge. There are six of these in Vedanta: perception (*pratyaksha*), inference (*anumAna*), scriptural or verbal testimony (*shabda* or *Agama shruti*), analogy (*upamAna*), presumption (*arthApatti*) and non-apprehension (*anupalabdhi*). The first three are the major ones referred to by Shankara.

prana (*prANa*, प्राण) – literally the 'breath of life'; the vital force in the body with which we identify in the 'vital sheath'.

prarabdha (*prArabdha*, प्रारब्ध) – This literally means 'begun' or 'undertaken'. It is the fruit of all of our past action that is now having its effect. This is one of the three types of sanskara. See agamin, sanchita, sanskara.

prasthana-traya (*prasthAna traya*, प्रस्थान त्रय) – *prasthAna* means 'system' or 'course' in the sense of a journey; *traya* just means 'threefold'. It refers to the three sources of knowledge of the Self: nyaya prasthana, sruti and smriti. See nyaya prasthana, shabda, sruti, smriti.

pratibhasa (noun) (*pratibhAsa*, प्रतिभास);

pratibhasika (adj.) (*prAtibhAsika*, प्रातिभासिक) – 'appearing or occurring to the mind', 'existing only in appearance', an illusion. See paramartha, vyavahara.

pratibimba-vada (*pratibimba vAda*, प्रतिबिम्ब वाद) – the theory that the jiva is a reflection of the Atman, similar to the reflection of an object in a mirror.

pratyaksha (*pratyakSha*, प्रत्यक्ष) – 'present before the eyes, clear, distinct etc.' but particularly 'direct perception or apprehension' as a valid source of knowledge. See pramana.

pratyaya (*pratyaya*, प्रत्यय) – belief, firm conviction, certainty; basis or cause of anything.

punya (*puNya*, पुण्य) – literally 'good' or 'virtuous'; used to refer to the 'reward' that accrues to us (according to the theory of karma) through the performing of unselfish actions. See also papa.

purna (*pUrNa*, पूर्ण) – full, complete, satisfied, perfect.

purushartha (*puruShArtha*, पुरुषार्थ) – the general meaning of this term is 'any object of human pursuit' but it is used here in the sense of human (i.e. self) effort to overcome 'fate', the fruit of one's past actions. See karma, sanskara.

purva (*pUrva,* पूर्व) – former, preceding.

purvapaksha (*pUrvapakSha,* पूर्वपक्ष) – the first objection to an assertion in any discussion or, more generally, the 'objector' in a debate.

purvamimamsa, (*pUrvamImAMsA,* पूर्वमीमांसा) – the philosophical system based upon the first part of the Vedas and attributed to Jaimini. It relates to enquiries into the nature of dharma or right action. See mimamsa, uttaramimamsa.

rajas (*rajas,* रजस्) – the second of the three gunas. Associated with animals and activity, emotions, desire, selfishness and passion. Adjective – rajassic or rajassika. See guna.

rishi (*RRiShi,* ऋषि) – author or singer of sacred Vedic hymns but now more generally used to refer to a saint or sage.

sadguru (*sadguru,* सद्गुरु) – the ultimate guru – one's own Self (*sat* = true, real). See guru.

sadhana (*sAdhana,* साधन) – literally 'leading straight to a goal'; refers to the spiritual disciplines followed as part of a 'path' towards Self-realization. See also chatushtaya sampatti.

saguna (*saguNa,* सगुण) – 'with qualities'. The term is usually used to refer to Brahman personified as the creator, Ishvara, to symbolize the most spiritual aspect of the world of appearances. See Brahman, Ishvara, nirguna.

sahaja sthiti (*sahaja sthiti,* सहज स्थिति) – Once Self-realization has been attained, there is full and lasting knowledge of the Self. '*sahaja*' means 'state' but this is not a state – it is our true nature. It is permanent ('*sthiti*' meaning 'steady' or 'remaining'), unlike the earlier stages of samadhi. See nirvikalpa, samadhi, savikalpa, vikalpa.

sakshibhava (*sAkshibhAva,* साक्षिभाव) – 'being or becoming' (*bhAva*) a 'witness' (*sAkshI*).

samadhana (*samAdhAna,* समाधान) – contemplation,

profound meditation; more usually translated as concentration; one of the 'six qualities' that form part of Shankara's chatushtaya sampatti. See chatushtaya sampatti.

samadhi (*samAdhi,* समाधि) – the state of total peace and stillness achieved during deep meditation. Several 'stages' are defined – see vikalpa, savikalpa samadhi, nirvikalpa samadhi and sahaja sthiti.

samhita (*saMhitA,* संहिता) – a philosophical or religious text constructed according to certain rules of sound. There are many of these in the Vedas. The reference in this book is in conjunction with the Astavakra Samhita or Gita. This book is not part of the Vedas. See Astavakra, gita.

Sankhya (*sAMkhya,* सांख्य) – one of the three main divisions of Indian philosophy and one of the six darshanas; attributed to Kapila.

sampradaya (*sampradAya,* सम्प्रदाय) – the tradition or established doctrine of teaching from master to pupil through the ages. *paramparA* refers to the general principle, whereas a *sampradAya* relates to a specific historical sage, such as Shankara. See also parampara.

samsara (*saMsAra,* संसार) – the cycle of death and rebirth, transmigration etc. to which we are supposedly subject in the phenomenal world until we become enlightened and escape. *saMsArI* – one who is bound to the cycle of birth and death.

samshaya (*saMshaya,* संशय) – uncertainty, irresolution, hesitation or doubt. See manana.

sanatana (*sanAtana,* सनातन) – literally 'eternal' or 'permanent'; in conjunction with dharma, this refers to our essential nature. The phrase *sanAtana dharma* is also used to refer to the traditional (also carrying the sense of 'original' and 'unadulterated') Hindu practices or as a synonym for 'Hinduism'. See dharma.

sanchita (*saMchita,* संचित) – one of the three types of sanskara, literally meaning 'collected' or 'piled up'. It refers to that sanskara which has been accumulated from past action but has still not manifested. See agamin, prarabdha, sanskara.

sanga *(sa~Nga,* सङ्ग*)* – assembly, association, company. See satsanga.

sanskara *(saMskAra,* संस्कार*)* – Whenever an action is performed with the desire for a specific result (whether for oneself or another), sanskara is created for that person. These accumulate and determine the situations with which we will be presented in the future and will influence the scope of future actions. There are three 'types' – agamin, sanchita and prarabdha. The accumulation of sanskara dictates the tendencies that we have to act in a particular way (vasanas). This is all part of the mechanism of karma. See agamin, karma, prarabdha, sanchita, vasana and karma.

sanyasa *(saMnyAsa,* संन्यास*)* – the final stage of the tradi-tional Hindu spiritual path; involves complete renunciation. The word literally means 'putting or throwing down, laying aside'; i.e. becoming an ascetic. One who does so is called a sanyasin *(saMnyAsin).* See also brahmacharya, grihasta, vanaprastha.

sat *(sat,* सत्*)* – existence, reality, truth (to mention a few). See also ananda, chit, satchitananda.

satchitananda *(sat - chit - Ananda* or *sachchidAnanda,* सच्चिदानन्द*)* – the oft-used word to describe our true nature, insofar as this can be put into words (which it can't). It translates as being-consciousness-bliss but see the separate bits for more detail.

satsanga *(satsa~Nga,* सत्सङ्ग*)* – association with the good; keeping 'good company'; most commonly used now to refer to a group of people gathered together to discuss (Advaita) philosophy or, increasingly, 'self-help'.

sattva *(sattva,* सत्त्व*)* – the highest of the three gunas. Associated with stillness, peace, truth, wisdom, unselfishness and spirituality, representing the highest aspirations of humankind. Adjective – sattvic or sattvika. See guna.

sattvapati *(sattvApatti,* सत्त्वापत्ति*)* – the (fourth) stage on a spiritual path, after which there is no longer any need for effort to be made (so called because there is now an abundance of sattva). *Apatti* means 'entering into a state or condition'.

satya (*satya,* सत्य) – true, real; *satyam* – truth.

savikalpa (*savikalpa,* सविकल्प) – (referring to samadhi) with division – still seeing the world as separate or different from oneself. See nirvikalpa, samadhi, vikalpa.

shabda (*shabda,* शब्द) – sound, word or speech. *shabda pramANa* – scriptural or verbal testimony. See pramana, nyaya prasthana, prasthana-traya, sruti, smriti.

shama (*shama,* शम) – literally tranquillity, absence of passion but more usually translated as mental discipline or self-control; one of the 'six qualities' that form part of Shankara's chatushtaya sampatti. See chatushtaya sampatti.

Shankara (*shaMkara,* शंकर) – eighth-century Indian philosopher responsible for firmly establishing the principles of Advaita. Though he died at an early age (32?), he commented on a number of major Upanishads, the Bhagavad Gita and the Brahmasutras, as well as being attributed as the author of a number of famous works, such as Atmabodha, Upadesha Sahasri and Vivekachudamani.

Shankaracharya (*shaMkarAchArya,* शंकराचार्य) – the title given to one of the teachers (see acharya) following the tradition in India established by Shankara (see Shankara). He established these positions, to be held by realized individuals who would take on the role of teacher and could be consulted by anyone having problems or questions of a spiritual nature.

sharira (*sharIra,* शरीर) – one's body divided into gross, subtle and causal aspects).

shastra (*shAstra,* शास्त्र) – order, teaching, instruction; any sacred book or composition that has divine authority.

shraddha (*shraddhA,* श्रद्धा) – faith, trust or belief (in the absence of direct personal experience); the student needs this initially in respect of what he or she is told by the guru or reads in the scriptures; one of the 'six qualities' that form part of Shankara's chatushtaya sampatti. See chatushtaya sampatti.

shravana (*shravaNa*, श्रवण) – hearing the truth from a sage or reading about it in such works as the Upanishads; first of the three key stages in the traditional spiritual path. See also manana, nididhyasana.

shruti (*shruti*, श्रुति) – refers to the Vedas, incorporating the Upanishads. Literally means 'hearing' and refers to the belief that the books contain orally transmitted, sacred wisdom from the dawn of time. See nyaya prasthana, pramana, smriti.

siddhanta (*siddhAnta*, सिद्धान्त) – final end or purpose; conclusion of an argument.

shubhecha (*shubhechChA*, शुभेच्छा) – 'good desire'; the initial impulse that starts us on a spiritual search. *shubha* means 'auspicious', 'good (in a moral sense)' and *ichChA* means 'wish', 'desire'.

smriti (*smRRiti*, स्मृति) – refers to material 'remembered' and subsequently written down. In practice, it mostly refers to books of law (in the sense of guidance for living) which were written and based upon the knowledge in the Vedas, i.e. the so-called dharma-shAstras – Manu, Yajnavalkya, Parashara. In the context of nyaya prasthana, it is used to refer to just one of these books – the Bhagavad Gita. See pramana, nyaya prasthana, sruti.

srishti-drishti-vada (*sRRiShTidRRiShTivAda*, सृष्टिदृष्टिवाद) – the theory that the world is separate from ourselves, having been created (by God or the big bang) and evolving independently of ourselves, i.e. the 'common sense' view of things. See also adhyasa, ajati, drishti-srishti-vada.

sthitaprajna (*sthitapraj~na*, स्थितप्रज्ञ) – meaning one 'standing' (*sthita*) in 'wisdom' (*prajna*); a person of steadiness and calm, firm in judgment, contented. The name is used in the Bhagavad Gita to refer to someone who is Self-realized.

sthula (*sthUla*, स्थूल) – large, thick, coarse, dense; the gross body (*sthUla sharIra*).

sukha (*sukha,* सुख) – comfortable, happy, prosperous etc. *sukham* – pleasure, happiness.

sushupti (*suShupti,* सुषुप्ति) – the deep-sleep state of consciousness. The 'sleeper ego' is called prajna. See also, jagrat, svapna, turiya.

svadharma (*svadharma,* स्वधर्म) – one's own dharma. See dharma.

svapna (*svapna,* स्वप्न) – the dream state of consciousness. The 'dreamer ego' is called taijasa. See also, jagrat, sushupti, turiya.

taijasa (*taijasa,* तैजस) – the 'dreamer ego' in the dream state of consciousness, svapna. See also vishva, prajna.

tamas (*tamas,* तमस्) – the 'lowest' of the three gunas. Associated with matter, and having characteristics such as inertia, laziness, heedlessness and death. Adjective – tamasic or tamasika. See guna.

tarka (*tarka,* तर्क) – reasoning, speculation, philosophical system or doctrine.

tarkika (*tArkika,* तार्किक) – logician or philosopher.

titiksha (*titikShA,* तितिक्षा) – forbearance or patience; one of the 'six qualities' that form part of Shankara's chatushtaya sampatti. See chatushtaya sampatti.

trikalatita (*trikAlAtIta,* त्रिकालातीत) – that which transcends past, present and future (describing the Self).

tripitaka (*tripiTaka,* त्रिपिटक) – the 'three baskets' or collections of sacred writings of the Buddhists viz. *sUtra, abhidharma, vinaya.*

turiya (*turIya,* तुरीय) – the 'fourth' state of consciousness (turiya means 'fourth'). It is actually not a state at all but our true nature, which is prevalent throughout the other three. The waker is not the dreamer is not the deep-sleeper but I am all three. See vishva, taijasa, prajna.

upadana (*upAdAna,* उपादान) – literally 'the act of taking for oneself'; used to refer to the 'material cause' in logic.

upadhi (*upAdhi,* उपाधि) – Literally, this means something that is put in place of another thing; a substitute, phantom or disguise. In Vedanta, it is commonly referred to as a 'limitation' or 'limiting adjunct' i.e. one of the 'identifications' made by ahankara that prevents us from realizing the Self.

upamana (*upamAna,* उपमान) – comparison, resemblance, analogy. One of the six pramanas.

upanishad (*upaniShat,* उपनिषत्) – one of the (108+) books forming part (usually the end) of one of the four Vedas. The parts of the word mean: to sit (*Shad*) near a master (*upa*) at his or her feet (*ni*), so that the idea is that we sit at the feet of a master to listen to his or her words. Monier-Williams (Ref. 5) states that, 'according to native authorities, upanishad means "setting at rest ignorance by revealing the knowledge of the supreme spirit"'. Note that the *d* changes to a *t* at the end of a word. See Vedanta.

uparama (*uparama,* उपरम) See uparati.

uparati (*uparati,* उपरति) – desisting from sensual enjoyment; 'reveling' in that which is 'near' i.e. one's own Self; also translated as following one's dharma or duty; one of the 'six qualities' that form part of Shankara's chatushtaya sampatti. See chatushtaya sampatti.

uttaramimamsa (*uttaramImAMsA,* उत्तरमीमांसा) – the Vedanta philosophy, based on the latter (uttara) part of the Vedas rather than the earlier (purva). Its founder was Badarayana, who authored the Brahmasutras. There are three main schools – dvaita, advaita and vishishtadvaita. See Brahmasutras, mimamsa, purvamimamsa, Veda.

vada (*vAda,* वाद) – speech, proposition, discourse, argument, discussion, explanation or exposition (of scriptures etc.)

vairagya (*vairAgya,* वैराग्य) – detachment or dispassion; indifference to the pleasure that results from success or the disappointment that results from failure. See sadhana, chatushtaya sampatti.

vaisheshika (*vaisheShika,* वैशेषिक) – one of the six classical Indian philosophies, a later development of nyaya by the theologian, Kanada; named after the nine 'essentially different substances' believed to constitute matter. See darshana, vishesha.

vanaprastha (*vanaprastha,* वनप्रस्थ) – the third stage of the traditional Hindu spiritual path, in which the Brahmin retires from life and becomes a 'forest dweller', living as a hermit. Traditionally speaking, 'a properly initiated *dvija* or twice-born'. See also brahmacharya, grihasta, sanyasa, vanaprastha.

vasana (*vAsanA,* वासना) – literally 'desiring' or 'wishing' – latent behavioral tendency in one's nature brought about through past action (karma) and the sanskara that resulted from this. See karma, sanskara.

Veda (*veda,* वेद) – knowledge, but the word is normally only used to refer to one of the four Vedas (see Vedanta) and vidya is used for knowledge per se. See vidya.

Vedanta (*vedAnta,* वेदान्त) – literally 'end' or 'culmination' (*anta*) of the Vedas. Veda in this context refers to the four Vedas, the Hindu equivalents of the Christian Bible (called Rig, *RRig* Veda; Sama, *sama* Veda; Atharva, *atharva* Veda; Yajur, *yajur* Veda). Traditionally, the last part of the Vedas is devoted to the Upanishads. See upanishad.

vidya (*vidyA,* विद्या) – knowledge, science, learning, philosophy. *Atma-vidyA* or *brahma-vidyA* is knowledge of the Self.

Vidyaranya (*vidyAraNya,* विद्यारण्य) – author of the Panchadashi (*pa~nchadashI*).

vikalpa (*vikalpa,* विकल्प) – doubt, uncertainty or indecision, division. See savikalpa, nirvikalpa, samadhi.

vikshepa (*vikShepa,* विक्षेप) – the 'projecting' power of maya. In the rope–snake metaphor, this superimposes the image of the snake upon the rope. See avarana, maya.

vinaya (*vinaya,* विनय) – the rules of discipline for Buddhist monks; school of Buddhist philosophy emphasizing conduct as the means to the end of suffering.

vishaya (*viShaya,* विषय) – object of sensory perception; any subject or topic; the subject of an argument.

vishesha (*visheSha,* विशेष) – literally 'distinction' or 'difference between'. The Vaisheshika philosophy believes that the material universe is made up of nine substances, each of which is 'essentially different' from any other. See Vaisheshika.

vishishta (*vishiShTa,* विशिष्ट) – distinguished, particular, excellent.

vishishtadvaita (*vishiShTAdvaita,* विशिष्टाद्वैत) – qualified non-dualism; the belief that God and the atman are distinct but not separate. Ramanuja is the scholar most often associated with this philosophy. See advaita, dvaita.

vishva (*vishva,* विश्व) – the 'waker ego' in the waking state of consciousness, jagrat. See also taijasa, prajna.

viveka (*viveka,* विवेक) – discrimination; the function of buddhi, having the ability to differentiate between the unreal and the real. See sadhana, chatushtaya sampatti.

vritti (*vRRitti,* वृत्ति) – In the context of Vedanta, this means a 'mood of the mind'. In general, it can mean a mode of conduct or behavior, character or disposition, business or profession etc, or simply a 'thought'. See aham vritti and idam vritti.

vyavahara (noun) (*vyavahAra,* व्यवहार);

vyavaharika (adj.), (*vyAvahArika,* व्यावहारिक) – the 'relative', 'empirical', or phenomenal world of appearances; the normal world in which we live and which we usually believe to be real; as opposed to paramarthika (real) and pratibhasika (illusory). See paramarthika and pratibhasika.

yoga (*yoga,* योग) – literally 'joining' or 'attaching' (our word 'yoke' derives from this). It is used generally to refer to any system whose aim is to 'join' our 'individual self' back to the 'universal Self'. The Yoga system pedantically refers to that specified by Patanjali and is one of the six Indian philosophical systems, closely associated with Sankhya. See bhakti, jnana, karma.

yuga (*yuga,* युग) – one of the four ages in the cycle of creation. See kalpa, kali yuga.

Appendix 1 Transliteration Schemes

Table 10 – Transliteration Schemes

Devana-gari	ITRANS	Roman	Velthuis	Harvard-Kyoto
अ	a	a	a	a
आ	aa or A	ā	aa or A	A
इ	i	i	i	i
ई	ii or I	ī	ii or I	I
ऋ	RRi or R^i	ṛ	.r	R
ॠ	RRI or R^I	ṝ	.R	q
ऌ	LLi or L^i	ḷ	.l	L
ॡ	LLI or L^I	ḹ	.L	E
उ	u	u	u	u

Devana-gari	ITRANS	Roman	Velthuis	Harvard-Kyoto
ऊ	uu or U	ū	uu or U	U
ए	e	e	e	e
ऐ	ai	ai	ai or E	ai
ओ	o	o	o	o
औ	au	au	au or O	au
ं	.n or .m or M	ṁ or ṃ	.m or M	M
ः	H	ḥ	.h or H	H
ख्	kh	kh	kh or K	kh
ग्	g	g	g	g
घ्	gh	gh	gh or G	gh
ङ्	~N	ṅ	¨n	G
च्	ch or c	c	c	c

Devana-gari	ITRANS	Roman	Velthuis	Harvard-Kyoto
छ्	Ch or chh	ch	ch or C	ch
ज्	j	j	j	j
झ्	jh	jh	jh or J	jh
क्	k	k	k	k
ञ्	~n	ñ	~n	J
ट्	T	ṭ	.t	T
ठ्	Th	ṭh	.th or .T	Th
ड्	D	ḍ	.d	D
ढ्	Dh	ḍh	.dh or .D	Dh
ण्	N	ṇ	.n	N
त्	t	t	t	t
थ्	th	th	th or T	th

Devana-gari	ITRANS	Roman	Velthuis	Harvard-Kyoto
छ्	d	d	d	d
ध्	dh	dh	dh or D	dh
न्	n	n	n	n
प्	p	p	p	p
फ्	ph	ph	ph or P	ph
ब्	b	b	b	b
भ्	bh	bh	bh or B	bh
म्	m	m	m	m
य्	y	y	y	y
र्	r	r	r	r
ल्	l	l	l	l
व्	v	v	v	v

Devana -gari	ITRANS	Roman	Velthuis	Harvard- Kyoto
श्	sh	ś	¨s	z
ष्	Sh or shh	ṣ	.s	S
स्	s	s	s	s
ह्	h	h	h	h

Note: The characters '.h' may also be added after any consonant in ITRANS to generate a *virAma*; however, since this will happen regardless if the consonant is not followed by a vowel, it is usually omitted. E.g. *k* is the same as *k.h*.

Appendix 2 Alternative Letter Forms

As has been noted in the text, some of the letters have two or more differing representations in Devanagari. A given source will normally be consistent in its use of a single variant but other traditions and books may use one of the alternative forms. E.g. the Monier-Williams dictionary uses the different variant of the letter *a*.

Table 11 – Alternative Letter Forms

Letter (ITRANS)	Usual Devanagari	Monier-Williams	SES
A	अ	ऄ	
RRi	ऋ		ऋृ
RRI	ॠ		ॠृ
E	ए		ए
Ai	ऐ		ऐ
Ch	छ		छ
jh	झ	र	झ
N	ण	ण	

Appendix 3 Vowel Forms, with and without Consonants

Table 12 – Vowel Forms

Vowel (ITRANS)	On Its Own	With Consonant	k + This Vowel
No vowel (virAma)	-	्	क्
a	अ	no change	क
A	आ	ा	का
i	इ	ि	कि
I	ई	ी	की
RRi	ऋ	ृ	कृ
RRI	ॠ	ॄ	कॄ
LLi	ऌ	no abbrev	कॢ
LLI	ॡ	no abbrev	कॣ
u	उ	ु	कु
U	ऊ	ू	कू
e	ए	े	के

ai	ऐ	◌ॅ	कै
o	ओ	◌ो	को
au	औ	◌ौ	कौ
aM	अं	◌ं	कं
aH	अः	◌ः	कः

Table 12 summarizes the use of vowels (+ *anusvAra* and *visarga*). Column 2 shows how they appear when used on their own or at the beginning of a word. Column 3 shows how their presence is signified when they appear after one or more consonants. Column 4 shows how the letter *k* appears when used with that vowel.

Appendix 4 Writing the Script

You will have to learn the alphabet if you wish to become sufficiently familiar with the forms of the letters to be able to read the words in the scriptures. This really means practicing writing the letters as well as reading them. You will have seen that the Devanagari reproduced in this book has been written in an italic script. Obviously it is not necessary to write it in this way in order for it to be understood. (But then this is, after all, the prime purpose of any written language.) However, if you are to learn the formally correct construction of each of the letters, you ought really to practice it as an exercise in calligraphy.

Unfortunately, an ordinary italic nib on a fountain pen or even in a calligraphy set is unlikely to be the correct shape. The edge of the nib should be angled. The pen is then tilted so that the edge is flush with the page as characters are written. This generates the necessary angular finish to the script. The nib must be cut away to the right for right-handed users and to the left for left-handed ones.

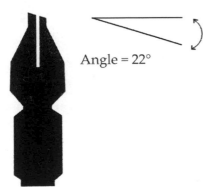

Angle = 22°

With care, an ordinary italic nib could be filed down in this way, finishing off with fine 'wet and dry' sandpaper. The width of nib depends upon the intended size of writing. If practicing only, a broad tip is probably best ($\approx$ 2.5mm); if you expect to write a lot at normal size, it will need to be narrower since the proportions of the letters are important. It is possible to obtain fountain pens with the correct nibs.

In the UK, fine or medium italic pens may be purchased from http://www.sanskritcourses.co.uk/. A number of books (including

Monier-Williams), CDs and a pack of Sanskrit Alphabet Cards may also be purchased here. (This latter is invaluable for helping you to learn the letters. You can also make them yourself from the freely downloadable Charles Wikner book mentioned above.)

The proportions of the letters can be seen by dividing them into three as shown below:

The order in which the parts of each letter are constructed will depend upon the source of instruction. I was taught (in England, by SES) that the top line of the letter should be constructed first in all cases except for *a*, where the left-hand part should be produced first. Next, any vertical line is drawn and finally, the key parts of the letter are drawn onto these. The American style insists that the distinctive part of each letter should be drawn first, then the vertical line, and the top line should always be done last, i.e. the exact opposite! Logically, the latter method seems more sensible, since you cannot know how long the top line should be until a word is complete. The Internet resources described earlier all recommend the latter style.

If you do seriously want to learn how to produce the script neatly and accurately, you should seek out a school or someone who is skilled in the art. This is really an exercise in calligraphy and cannot easily be learned from a book. If you are not interested in strict accuracy, just get yourself an appropriate pen and modify the nib as shown above. (While searching for sites earlier, I came across one which suggested that a right-handed person could use a left-hand italic pen. Presumably the reverse also applies. I do not know first hand how well this might work.) Then practice producing the letters in whichever way you like until you get a result that you find acceptable. Finally, if you are not interested at all in the calligraphy element and are unconcerned if the letter proportions are not strictly accurate, just dig out an old fountain pen or even a felt-tip or ballpoint and practice. Above all, however, *practice*. This will prove invaluable in helping you to learn the alphabet.

Appendix 5 Answer to Final Example

सर्वे भवन्तु सुखिनः सर्वे सन्तु निरामयाः ।
सर्वे भद्राणि पश्यन्तु मा कश्चिद् दुःखभाग्भवेत् ॥

sarve bhavantu sukhinaH sarve santu nirAmayAH .
sarve bhadrANi pashyantu mA kashchid duHkhabhAgbhavet
..

Let everyone be happy; let them be free from illness.
May they experience prosperity and let sorrow not be the lot
of anyone.

Bibliography

1. Transliteration of Devanāgarī, D. Wujastyk, 1996 http://indology.info/email/members/wujastyk/. No ISBN.
2. A Practical Sanskrit Introductory, Charles Wikner, 1966. No ISBN.
3. *laghusiddhAntakaumudI* – The Laws of Grammar: A Short Elucidation, School of Economic Science, 1997. No ISBN.
4. *devavANIpraveshikA* – An Introduction to the Sanskrit Language, Robert P. Goldman and Sally J. Sutherland, Center for South and Southeast Asia Studies, University of California, Berkeley, 1987. No ISBN.
5. A Sanskrit English Dictionary, M. Monier-Williams, Motilal Banarsidass, 1995. ISBN 81-208-0065-6.
6. Introduction to Sanskrit Part 1, Thomas Egenes, Motilal Banarsidass, 1989. ISBN 978-81-208-1140-9. This is also available electronically at http://www.scribd.com/doc/32874508/Introduction-to-Sanskrit-by-Thomas-Egenes.
7. Introduction to Sanskrit Part 2, Thomas Egenes, Motilal Banarsidass, 1999. ISBN 978-81-208-1693-0.
8. Sanskrit Manual: A quick-reference guide to the phonology and grammar of Classical Sanskrit, Roderick S. Bucknell, Motilal Banarsidass, 1994. ISBN 81-208-1188-7.
9. The Student's English-Sanskrit Dictionary, Vaman Shivram Apte, Motilal Banarsidass, 1920. ISBN 81-208-0299-3.
10. A Concise Dictionary of Indian Philosophy: Sanskrit terms defined in English, John Grimes, Indica Books, 2009. ISBN 81-86569-80-4.
11. The Wonder That Is Sanskrit, Sampad and Vijay, Sri Aurobindo Society Pondicherry, 2002. ISBN 1-890206-50-4.
12. Language and Truth: A study of the Sanskrit language and its relationship with principles of truth, Paul Douglas, Shepheard-Walwyn, 2010. ISBN 978-0-85683-271-0.

13. The Four Quartets, T. S. Eliot, Faber and Faber, 1944. ISBN 0-571-04994-X.

14. The Bhagavad Gita, Winthrop Sargeant, State Universtity of New York Press, 1994. ISBN 0-87395-830-6.

15. Bhagavad Gita, Nitya Chaitanya Yati, D. K. Printworld (P) Ltd, 1981. ISBN 81-246-0010-4.

16. Srimad Bhagavad Gita, Kailash Nath Kalia, New Age Books, 2008. ISBN 978-81-7822-306-3.

Index

Note: **bold** page number = main entry;
italic page number = definition

**MANTRA
BOOKS**

We publish books on Eastern religions and philosophies.
Books that aim to inform and explore the various
traditions, that began rooted in East and
have migrated West.